Management Accounting: Budgeting

Level 4

Professional Diploma in Accounting

Question Bank

Third edition 2018

ISBN 9781 5097 1878 8

British Library Cataloguing-in-Publication Data
A catalogue record for this book is available from the British Library

Published by

BPP Learning Media Ltd
BPP House, Aldine Place
142-144 Uxbridge Road
London W12 8AA

www.bpp.com/learningmedia

Printed in the United Kingdom

Your learning materials, published by BPP Learning Media Ltd, are printed on paper obtained from traceable sustainable sources.

The contents of this course material are intended as a guide and not professional advice. Although every effort has been made to ensure that the contents of this course material are correct at the time of going to press, BPP Learning Media makes no warranty that the information in this course material is accurate or complete and accept no liability for any loss or damage suffered by any person acting or refraining from acting as a result of the material in this course material.

We are grateful to the AAT for permission to reproduce the sample assessment(s). The answers to the sample assessment(s) have been published by the AAT. All other answers have been prepared by BPP Learning Media Ltd.

A note about copyright

Dear Customer

What does the little © mean and why does it matter?

Your market-leading BPP books, course materials and e-learning materials do not write and update themselves. People write them on their own behalf or as employees of an organisation that invests in this activity. Copyright law protects their livelihoods. It does so by creating rights over the use of the content.

Breach of copyright is a form of theft – as well as being a criminal offence in some jurisdictions, it is potentially a serious breach of professional ethics.

With current technology, things might seem a bit hazy but, basically, without the express permission of BPP Learning Media:

- Photocopying our materials is a breach of copyright
- Scanning, ripcasting or conversion of our digital materials into different file formats, uploading them to Facebook or e-mailing them to your friends is a breach of copyright

You can, of course, sell your books, in the form in which you have bought them – once you have finished with them. (Is this fair to your fellow students? We update for a reason.) Please note the e-products are sold on a single user licence basis: we do not supply 'unlock' codes to people who have bought them secondhand.

And what about outside the UK? BPP Learning Media strives to make our materials available at prices students can afford by local printing arrangements, pricing policies and partnerships which are clearly listed on our website. A tiny minority ignore this and indulge in criminal activity by illegally photocopying our material or supporting organisations that do. If they act illegally and unethically in one area, can you really trust them?

Contents

Introduction

This is BPP Learning Media's AAT Question Bank for *Management Accounting: Budgeting*. It is part of a suite of ground-breaking resources produced by BPP Learning Media for AAT assessments.

This Question Bank has been written in conjunction with the BPP Course Book, and has been carefully designed to enable students to practise all of the learning outcomes and assessment criteria for the units that make up *Management Accounting: Budgeting*. It is fully up to date as at June 2017 and reflects both the AAT's qualification specification and the sample assessments provided by the AAT.

This Question Bank contains these key features:

- Tasks corresponding to each chapter of the Course Book. Some tasks are designed for learning purposes, others are of assessment standard
- AAT's AQ2016 sample assessment 1 and answers for *Management Accounting: Budgeting* and further BPP practice assessments

The emphasis in all tasks and assessments is on the practical application of the skills acquired.

Approaching the assessment

When you sit the assessment it is very important that you follow the on screen instructions. This means you need to carefully read the instructions, both on the introduction screens and during specific tasks.

When you access the assessment you should be presented with an introductory screen with information similar to that shown below (taken from the introductory screen from one of the AAT's AQ2016 sample assessments for *Management Accounting: Budgeting*).

> We have provided this **sample assessment** to help you familiarise yourself with our e-assessment environment. It is designed to demonstrate as many of the question types that you may find in a live assessment as possible. It is not designed to be used on its own to determine whether you are ready for a live assessment.
>
> At the end of this sample assessment you will receive an immediate assessment result. This will only take into account your responses to tasks 1, 2, 3, 5, 6 and 7 as these are the elements of the assessment that are computer marked. In the live assessment, your responses to tasks 4 and 8 will be human marked.

Assessment information:

You have **2 hours and 30 minutes** to complete this sample assessment.

This assessment contains **8 tasks** and you should attempt to complete **every** task.
Each task is independent. You will not need to refer to your answers to previous tasks.
Read every task carefully to make sure you understand what is required.

Where the date is relevant, it is given in the task data.
Both minus signs and brackets can be used to indicate negative numbers **unless** task instructions say otherwise.

You must use a full stop to indicate a decimal point. For example, write 100.57 NOT 100,57 or 100 57
You may use a comma to indicate a number in the thousands, but you don't have to. For example, 10000 and 10,000 are both acceptable.

The actual instructions will vary depending on the subject you are studying for. It is very important you read the instructions on the introductory screen and apply them in the assessment. You don't want to lose marks when you know the correct answer just because you have not entered it in the right format.

In general, the rules set out in the AAT sample assessments for the subject you are studying for will apply in the real assessment, but you should carefully read the information on this screen again in the real assessment, just to make sure. This screen may also confirm the VAT rate used if applicable.

A full stop is needed to indicate a decimal point. We would recommend using minus signs to indicate negative numbers and leaving out the comma signs to indicate thousands, as this results in a lower number of key strokes and less margin for error when working under time pressure. Having said that, you can use whatever is easiest for you as long as you operate within the rules set out for your particular assessment.

You have to show competence throughout the assessment and you should therefore complete all of the tasks. Don't leave questions unanswered.

In some assessments, written or complex tasks may be human marked. In this case you are given a blank space or table to enter your answer into. You are told in the assessments which tasks these are (note that there may be none if all answers are marked by the computer).

If these involve calculations, it is a good idea to decide in advance how you are going to lay out your answers to such tasks by practising answering them on a word document, and certainly you should try all such tasks in this Question Bank and in the AAT's environment using the sample assessments.

When asked to fill in tables, or gaps, never leave any blank even if you are unsure of the answer. Fill in your best estimate.

Note that for some assessments where there is a lot of scenario information or tables of data provided (eg tax tables), you may need to access these via 'pop-ups'. Instructions will be provided on how you can bring up the necessary data during the assessment.

Finally, take note of any task specific instructions once you are in the assessment. For example you may be asked to enter a date in a certain format or to enter a number to a certain number of decimal places.

Grading

To achieve the qualification and to be awarded a grade, you must pass all the mandatory unit assessments, all optional unit assessments (where applicable) and the synoptic assessment.

The AAT Level 4 Professional Diploma in Accounting will be awarded a grade. This grade will be based on performance across the qualification. Unit assessments and synoptic assessments are not individually graded. These assessments are given a mark that is used in calculating the overall grade.

How overall grade is determined

You will be awarded an overall qualification grade (Distinction, Merit, and Pass). If you do not achieve the qualification you will not receive a qualification certificate, and the grade will be shown as unclassified.

The marks of each assessment will be converted into a percentage mark and rounded up or down to the nearest whole number. This percentage mark is then weighted according to the weighting of the unit assessment or synoptic assessment within the qualification. The resulting weighted assessment percentages are combined to arrive at a percentage mark for the whole qualification.

Grade definition	Percentage threshold
Distinction	90–100%
Merit	80–89%
Pass	70–79%
Unclassified	0–69% Or failure to pass one or more assessment/s

Re-sits

The AAT Professional Diploma In Accounting is not subject to re-sit restrictions.

You should only be entered for an assessment when you are well prepared and you expect to pass the assessment.

AAT qualifications

The material in this book may support the following AAT qualifications:

AAT Professional Diploma in Accounting Level 4, AAT Professional Diploma in Accounting at SCQF Level 8 and Certificate: Accounting (Level 5 AATSA).

Supplements

From time to time we may need to publish supplementary materials to one of our titles. This can be for a variety of reasons. From a small change in the AAT unit guidance to new legislation coming into effect between editions.

You should check our supplements page regularly for anything that may affect your learning materials. All supplements are available free of charge on our supplements page on our website at:

www.bpp.com/learning-media/about/students

Improving material and removing errors

There is a constant need to update and enhance our study materials in line with both regulatory changes and new insights into the assessments.

From our team of authors BPP appoints a subject expert to update and improve these materials for each new edition.

Their updated draft is subsequently technically checked by another author and from time to time non-technically checked by a proof reader.

We are very keen to remove as many numerical errors and narrative typos as we can but given the volume of detailed information being changed in a short space of time we know that a few errors will sometimes get through our net.

We apologise in advance for any inconvenience that an error might cause. We continue to look for new ways to improve these study materials and would welcome your suggestions. If you have any comments about this book, please email nisarahmed@bpp.com or write to Nisar Ahmed, AAT Head of Programme, BPP Learning Media Ltd, BPP House, Aldine Place, London W12 8AA.

Question Bank

Chapter 1 – Cost classification and behaviour

Task 1.1

Match the departments in the first column with their purpose in the second column. *(CBT instructions: Click on a box in the left column, then on one in the right column. To remove a line, click on it.)*

Department
Sales team
Finance department
Facilities team
HR department
Marketing team

Purpose
Prepares the draft financial statements of the organisation
Ensures the business manages its staff correctly, including adhering to employment law
Promotes the organisation in the market place
Finds and secures new customers
Responsible for decisions concerning the buildings from which the organisation trades

Task 1.2

Cost	Budget
Market research survey	▼
Wages of factory workers	▼
Recruitment advertisement for a new finance director in an accountancy magazine	▼
Raw material costs	▼
Salary of marketing director	▼

Picklist:

Administrative overheads budget
Marketing budget
Production budget

Task 1.3

Match the functions listed below to the appropriate department.

Function	Department
Prepares accounting information, pays suppliers and staff, chases customers for payment etc	▼
Recruits, develops and disciplines staff, and ensures that employment law is followed by the business	▼
Buys raw materials for use in the production process	▼
Makes sales to new and existing customers	▼
Investigates and responds to customer complaints	▼

Picklist:

After-sales service team
Finance department
HR department
Purchasing team
Sales team

Task 1.4

Allocate the following costs to the responsibility centres in a business.

Costs	Responsibility centre
Client entertaining at horse racing	▼
Repair of security alarm system in offices	▼
Sick pay for production manager	▼
Bonus for sales managers	▼
Depreciation of production equipment	▼

Picklist:

Administration department
HR (Personnel) department
Marketing department
Production department
Sales team

Task 1.5

A company is hosting a dinner event at a function room to entertain clients and is creating the budget for the cost.

Classify each of the costs below in terms of its behaviour as semi-variable, variable, stepped or fixed.

Cost	Behaviour
Room hire	▼
Food for attendees	▼
Hire of waiting staff – 1 required per 20 attendees	▼

Picklist:

Fixed
Semi-variable
Stepped
Variable

Task 1.6

Match each type of cost in the first column with the correct type of expenditure in the second column. *(CBT instructions: Click on a box in the left column, then on one in the right column. To remove a line, click on it.)*

Cost
Computer hardware servers
Wages for production staff
Replacement of worn floor tiles
Repairs to the factory roof
Upgrade of a machine, extending its useful life

Expenditure
Capital
Revenue

Task 1.7

At a production level of 20,000 units a production cost totals £128,000. At a production level of 32,000 units the same cost totals £204,800.

This a variable cost.

True ☐

False ☐

Task 1.8

From the list below, drag and drop the most appropriate method of apportioning the overheads given in the table between two production departments.

Drag and drop choices:

Average inventory of raw materials held
Floor area
Number of staff employed
Units produced

Cost	Apportionment basis
Heating	
Rental on storage unit for raw materials	
Canteen expenses	
Depreciation of factory building	

Task 1.9

The following details are available for four types of cost at three activity levels:

	Cost at 10,000 units	Cost at 20,000 units	Cost at 25,000 units
Cost 1	18,000	18,000	18,000
Cost 2	30,000	60,000	60,000
Cost 3	30,000	60,000	75,000
Cost 4	20,000	30,000	35,000

Classify each cost by behaviour (semi-variable, variable, stepped or fixed).

	Cost behaviour
Cost 1	▼
Cost 2	▼
Cost 3	▼
Cost 4	▼

Picklist:

Fixed
Semi-variable
Stepped
Variable

Task 1.10

A manufacturing business anticipates that its variable production costs and fixed production costs will be £23,000 and £15,000 respectively at a production level of 10,000 units.

Complete the table to show the budgeted total production cost and the budgeted cost per unit at each of the activity levels. Give the cost per unit to 2 decimal places.

Activity level (units)	Budgeted total production cost £	Budgeted cost per unit £
8,000		
12,000		
15,000		

Task 1.11

Given below are a number of types of cost.

Classify each one according to its behaviour (semi-variable, variable, stepped or fixed).

	Cost behaviour
Maintenance contract which costs £10,000 annually plus an average of £500 cost per call out	▼
Sales car depreciation based upon miles travelled	▼
Machine consumables cost based on machine hours	▼
Rent for a building that houses the factory, stores and maintenance departments	▼

Picklist:

Fixed
Semi-variable
Stepped
Variable

Task 1.12

Drag and drop an appropriate accounting treatment for each of the costs in the table below.

Costs	Accounting treatment
Servicing of office computer equipment	
Materials wastage in production process	
Depreciation of marketing director's car	
Bonus for finance director	
Sick pay for production workers	

Drag and drop choices:

Allocate to administrative overheads
Allocate to marketing overheads
Charge to production in a labour hour overhead rate
Direct cost

Task 1.13

A business produces one product in its factory which has two production departments, cutting and finishing. There is one service department, stores, which spends 80% of its time servicing the cutting department and the remainder servicing the finishing department.

The expected costs of producing 50,000 units in the following quarter are as follows:

Direct materials	£16.00 per unit
Direct labour	3 hours cutting @ £7.50 per hour
	2 hours finishing @ £6.80 per hour
Cutting overheads	£380,000
Finishing overheads	£280,000
Stores overheads	£120,000

It is estimated that in each of the cost centres 60% of the overheads are variable and the remainder are fixed.

Determine the budgeted cost per unit of production (in £ to the nearest penny) under the following costing methods.

(i) Absorption costing – fixed and variable overheads are to be absorbed on a direct labour hour basis

£	

(ii) Marginal costing

£	

Task 1.14

Drampton plc, a computer retailer, has recently taken over Little Ltd, a small company making personal computers (PCs) and servers. Little appears to make all of its profits from servers. Drampton's finance director tells you that Little's fixed overheads are currently charged to production using standard labour hours and gives you their standard cost of making PCs and servers. These are shown below.

Little Ltd: Standard cost per computer

Model	Server	PC
Annual budgeted volume	5	5,000
Unit standard cost		
	£	£
Material and labour	50,000	500
Fixed overhead	4,000	40
Standard cost per unit	54,000	540

The finance director asks for your help and suggests you reclassify the fixed overheads between the two models using activity-based costing. You are given the following information.

Budgeted total annual fixed overheads

	£
Set-up costs	10,000
Rent and power (production area)	120,000
Rent (stores area)	50,000
Salaries of store issue staff	40,000
Total	220,000

Every time Little makes a server, it has to stop making PCs and rearrange the factory layout. The cost of this is shown as set-up costs. If the factory did not make any servers, these costs would be eliminated.

Cost drivers

	Server	PC	Total
Number of set-ups	5	0	5
Number of weeks of production	10	40	50
Floor area of stores (square metres)	400	400	800
Number of issues of inventory	2,000	8,000	10,000

Prepare a note for Drampton's finance director. In the note, you should use the cost drivers to reallocate Little's budgeted total fixed annual overheads between server and PC production and so complete the following.

NOTE

To: Drampton's finance director
From: Accounting technician
Date: 7 August 20X5
Subject: **Little Ltd – treatment of fixed overheads**

Introduction

	Allocated overheads to Server £	Allocated overheads to PC £
Set-up costs		
Rent and power (production area)		
Rent (stores area)		
Salaries of store issue staff		

ABC workings

Chapter 2 – Forecasting data

Task 2.1

Match each type of data in the first column with an appropriate source for it in the second column. *(CBT instructions: Click on a box in the left column, then on one in the right column. To remove a line, click on it.)*

Data
The previous year's financial statements for a competitor company
Previous month's discounts allowed
Industry average profit margin
Information about a competitor's success
Average sick days of employees per month

Source
Financial press
Companies House
HR department
Trade association
Internal accounting records

Task 2.2

Which of the following sets of data is required when preparing the labour usage budget?

Select from:

	✓
Forecast labour hours per unit and labour cost per hour	
Forecast production units and labour cost per unit	
Forecast sales units and labour hours per unit	
Forecast production units and labour hours per unit	

Task 2.3

If the materials cost per kg and the materials usage budget are already forecast, which other piece of information is required to construct the materials purchases budget?

Select from:

	✓
Production budget	
Opening and closing inventory of finished goods	
Sales budget	
Opening and closing inventory of raw materials	

Task 2.4

Forecasting is an important technique for budgeting purposes, however, it has limitations.

Explain the general limitations of forecasting.

Task 2.5

Analysis of historical sales data shows a growth trend of 3.5% per quarter. The sales in quarter 1 were 122,000 units.

The time series analysis has also indicated the following seasonal variations:

Quarter 1	+ 6,000 units
Quarter 2	– 8,000 units
Quarter 3	+12,000 units
Quarter 4	–10,000 units

The forecast sales in units (to the nearest whole unit) for the remaining three quarters are:

Quarter	Forecast sales (units)
Quarter 2	
Quarter 3	
Quarter 4	

Task 2.6

The trend figures for sales in units for a business for the four quarters of last year are given below:

Quarter 1	320,000
Quarter 2	325,000
Quarter 3	330,000
Quarter 4	335,000

The seasonal variations are expressed as follows:

Quarter 1	–18%
Quarter 2	+21%
Quarter 3	+7%
Quarter 4	–10%

What are the forecast sales for each of the quarters of next year?

Quarter	Forecast sales (units)
Quarter 1	
Quarter 2	
Quarter 3	
Quarter 4	

Task 2.7

What are the limitations of using time series analysis to forecast figures?

Task 2.8

(a) Explain the five stages of the product life cycle and how costs and income will alter in each of the five stages.

(b) How does knowledge of the product life cycle affect forecasting of future sales?

Task 2.9

At which stage in the product life cycle is time series analysis most likely to produce a fairly accurate figure for future sales?

Select from:

	✓
Development	
Launch	
Growth	
Maturity	
Decline	

Task 2.10

The production and sales in units for a business for the next six months are as follows:

	Jan	Feb	Mar	Apr	May	June
Production – units	3,600	2,900	3,200	3,100	3,400	4,000
Sales – units	3,500	3,000	3,000	3,200	3,500	3,800

The variable production costs are £10.50 per unit and the variable selling costs are £3.80 per unit.

Complete the following (to the nearest £).

	Jan	Feb	Mar	Apr	May	Jun
Forecast variable production costs £						
Forecast variable selling costs £						

Task 2.11

The direct materials cost for Quarter 1 and Quarter 2 of next year have been estimated in terms of current prices as £657,000 and £692,500 respectively. The current price index for these materials is 126.4 and the price index is estimated as 128.4 for Quarter 1 of next year and 131.9 for Quarter 2.

Complete the following (to the nearest £).

	Quarter 1	Quarter 2
Forecast direct materials costs £		

Task 2.12

The production and sales levels for the next three months are estimated as follows:

	Jan	Feb	Mar
Production – units	4,200	4,400	4,500
Sales – units	4,100	4,300	4,650

Variable production costs are currently £25.00 per unit and variable selling costs are £8.00 per unit. The price indices for the production costs and selling costs are currently 135.2 and 140.5 respectively.

The anticipated price indices for production and selling costs for the next three months are given below:

	Jan	Feb	Mar
Production costs index	137.3	139.0	139.6
Selling costs index	141.5	143.0	143.7

Complete the following (to the nearest £).

	Jan	Feb	Mar
Forecast variable production costs £			
Forecast variable selling costs £			

Task 2.13

Last month, a company's electricity bill was £35,000. The cost of electricity will increase with RPI in the coming month, but a prompt payment discount of 5% has also been negotiated.

Last month's machinery maintenance costs were £20,000 when the company had to make 4 call-outs to specialist engineers. The engineers predict that two more machines will fail and require a call-out each in the coming month. Due to rising fuel costs, the cost of a call-out will increase by 5% next month.

Last month's water costs were £62,000 but were unusually high due to a burst pipe (now fixed), which contributed £15,000 to the costs last month. Water prices increase with RPI each month.

The RPI for the last month was 224.6 and the RPI for the coming month is predicted to be 240.3.

The forecast total electricity, machinery maintenance and water costs for the coming month (to the nearest whole number) are

£	

Task 2.14

Last year's rent was £65,000 but will increase next year by 5.5%.

Last year's insurance premium was £15,700 but will increase next year by 10%.

Last year's power costs were £84,000 and these normally increase in line with the average RPI each year.

The average RPI for last year was 166.3 and it is believed that the average RPI for next year will be 171.2.

The forecast fixed costs for next year (to the nearest whole number) are

£	

Task 2.15

The costs of a factory maintenance department appear to be partially dependent upon the number of machine hours operated each month. The machine hours and the maintenance department costs for the last six months are given below:

	Machine hours	Maintenance cost £
June	14,200	285,000
July	14,800	293,000
August	15,200	300,000
September	14,500	290,000
October	15,000	298,000
November	14,700	292,000

The estimated variable cost per machine hour is

£	

The estimated fixed costs of the maintenance department are

£	

Task 2.16

The activity levels and related production costs for the last six months were as follows:

	Activity level units	Production cost £
July	63,000	608,000
August	70,000	642,000
September	76,000	699,000
October	73,000	677,000
November	71,000	652,000
December	68,000	623,000

Complete the following, using the high low method to determine the fixed element of the production costs and the variable rate.

State which of the two estimates is likely to be the most accurate and why.

Forecast units	Production costs £
74,000	
90,000	

Task 2.17

Explain the following sample methods and give an example of the circumstances in which each might be used and the sample would be chosen.

(i) Random sampling
(ii) Stratified sampling

Chapter 3 – Budgetary control systems

Task 3.1

Explain what a budget is, and how it can help management perform their duties.

Task 3.2

For each scenario given below, select the option which best describes the purpose for which the budget is being used in the scenario.

Scenario	Budget use
In order to meet a profit target, the managing director reduces the figure in next year's budget for the staff Christmas party by 25%	▼
The sales director divides the costs for client entertainment between his two sales teams, and gives the managers of those teams permission to spend within that level	▼
A retail company is wishing to expand its operations and so includes the rental costs of new shops in its budget	▼
The purchasing manager informs the production manager there will be a world-wide shortage of one type of material in the coming period. The production manager budgets for a different product mix because of this.	▼

Picklist:

Authorisation
Co-ordination
Cost control
Planning

Task 3.3

Briefly explain each of the following terms.

Budget committee
Budget holders
Budget manual
Master budget

Task 3.4

Explain the procedures that will be followed from the start of the budgeting process through to the completion of the master budget.

Task 3.5

You are the accountant at a manufacturing business, where the managing director already thinks the annual budgeting process wastes too much management time.

Explain to the managing director why it may be appropriate to use a rolling budget and how this works.

Task 3.6

You are the new accountant at a manufacturing business. The managing director wants the time spent on preparing the budget to be kept to a minimum. He wants the costs in last year's budget to be adjusted to reflect inflation of costs, and no further work to be done. This is what has been done every year for the last three years.

You discover that some costs included in the budget are always exceeded in practice and so the budget is ignored by some managers.

Write a memo to the managing director explaining why this method of budgeting may be inappropriate, and suggesting an alternative.

Task 3.7

Draft budgets have been prepared by the accounts department of H Ltd based on the results of the previous two years. Budgets are prepared annually and reviewed at the year end. Jai Barry, the Managing Director of H Ltd, is concerned that there is a lack of involvement of the departmental managers in the budgeting process that is leading to poor performances. She has asked you whether other types of budgeting might be more suitable for the company and to explain how these would help to involve the production and sales departments in preparing the forecasts.

Write an email to Jai Barry that:

(a) Briefly explains how the company's budgeting procedures could be improved by using:

(i) Departmental budgets
(ii) Rolling budgets

(b) Explains TWO methods of motivating managers to be more involved in preparing the budgets.

Task 3.8

Prepare a report explaining how budgets can be used as a tool to motivate managers.

To: Managing Director	**Date:**
From:	**Subject:** Motivating managers

Chapter 4 – Budget preparation

Task 4.1

A business has budgeted sales for the next period of 13,800 units of its product. The inventory at the start of the period is 2,100 units and this is to be reduced to 1,500 units at the end of the period.

Which of the following is the production quantity in units for the period?

Select from:

	✓
13,800	
13,200	
14,400	
2,100	
1,500	

Task 4.2

A business is preparing its production budget for the next quarter. It is estimated that 200,000 units of the product can be sold in the quarter and the opening inventory is currently 35,000 units. The inventory level is to be reduced by 30% by the end of the quarter.

Which of the following is the production budget in units for the quarter?

Select from:

	✓
189,500	
175,500	
210,500	
191,923	

Task 4.3

A business is preparing its production budget for the next quarter. It will have opening inventory of 1,500 units but wants no closing inventory at the end of the quarter. Sales are likely to exceed production by 20%.

Which of the following is the production budget for the quarter?

Select from:

	✓
1,500 units	
1,875 units	
7,500 units	
9,000 units	

Task 4.4

A production process has normal losses of 3% of completed output and production of 16,200 good units is required.

How many units must be produced in total?

Select from:

	✓
16,686	
16,702	
16,486	
15,714	

Task 4.5

The opening inventory and period sales for units of Product A are shown below. Closing inventory is to be 25% of the next period's sales. Sales in period 4 will be 11,200 units.

Complete the production budget for Product A in units.

	Period 1	Period 2	Period 3
Opening inventory	2,700		
Production			
Subtotal			
Sales	10,800	11,500	11,000
Closing inventory			

Task 4.6

The production budget for a product X is shown below for the next three months.

Quality control procedures have shown that 4% of completed production are found to be defective and are unsellable.

Complete the following, showing how many units of product X must be manufactured to allow for the defective items.

	Period 1	Period 2	Period 3
Required units	12,000	11,000	12,500
Manufactured units			

Task 4.7

A business requires 25,400 units of production in a period and each unit requires 5 kg of raw materials in the finished product. The production process has a normal loss of 10% of raw materials during the production process.

What is the total amount of the raw material required for the period?

Select from:

	✓
114,300 kg	
26,950 kg	
28,222 kg	
141,112 kg	

Task 4.8

The production budget for the product is 40,000 units in the quarter.

Each unit of product requires 5 kgs of raw material. Opening inventory of raw material is budgeted to be 30,000 kg and inventory levels are to be reduced by 20% by the end of the quarter.

The material usage budget for the raw material is ______ kgs.

The materials purchasing budget for the raw material is ______ kgs.

Task 4.9

The production budget in units for the next period, period 1, is 32,000, and for period 2 is 35,000.

Each completed unit of the product requires 8 kgs of raw material; however, the production process has a normal loss of 20% of material. Inventory levels of raw materials are held in order to be sufficient to cover 25% of gross production for the following period. The inventory of raw material at the start of period 1 is budgeted to be 64,000 kgs.

The price of each kilogram of raw material is £2.50.

Complete the following.

	Period 1
Materials usage budget in kg	
Materials purchases budget in kg	
Materials purchases budget in £	

Task 4.10

A product requires 18 labour hours for each unit. However, 10% of working hours are non-productive.

How many hours must an employee be paid for in order to produce 20 units?

Select from:

	✓
324 hours	
400 hours	
396 hours	
360 hours	

Task 4.11

A business wishes to produce 120,000 units of its product with a standard labour time of 4 hours per unit. The workforce are currently working at 120% efficiency.

How many hours will it take to produce the units required?

Select from:

	✓
400,000 hours	
384,000 hours	
100,000 hours	
480,000 hours	

Task 4.12

	Quarter 1	Quarter 2
Budgeted sales	102,000 units	115,000 units

The inventory of finished goods at the start of quarter 1 is 17,000 units and it is business policy to maintain closing finished goods inventory levels at one-sixth of the following quarter's budgeted sales.

Each unit is forecast to take 5.5 labour hours, however, it is anticipated that during quarter 1, due to technical problems, the workforce will only be working at 95% efficiency.

You are to produce the production budget and the labour usage budget for quarter 1.

For quarter 1, the production budget is [ ] units.

For quarter 1, the labour usage budget is [ ] hours.

Task 4.13

Using the information given below complete the following budgets for period 1.

	Period 1
Sales budget (£)	
Production budget (units)	
Materials usage budget (kg)	
Materials purchasing budget (kg)	
Labour budget (hours)	
Labour budget (£)	

The sales forecast for period 1 is 3,000 units and for period 2 is 3,400 units. The selling price will be £40 per unit.

The closing inventory of finished goods is to be enough to cover 20% of sales demand for the next period.

3% of production is defective and has to be scrapped with no scrap value.

Each unit of production requires 4 kgs of raw material X and the production process has a normal loss of 10% of the materials input into the process.

It is policy to hold enough raw materials inventory to cover 35% of the following period's production. The inventory level at the start of period 1 is 4,200 kgs of raw material. The material usage for production in period 2 is budgeted as 16,040 kgs.

The standard time for production of one unit is 2 labour hours, however, due to necessary break times only 80% of the time worked is productive. The labour force are paid at a rate of £8 per hour.

Task 4.14

The data provided by the sales and production departments for two products is as follows:

	Aye	Bee
Budgeted sales (units) quarter 1	1,500	2,400
Budgeted sales (units) quarter 2	1,500	2,400
Budgeted material per unit (kg)	4	7
Budgeted labour hours per unit	10	7
Opening units of finished inventory	160	300
Closing units of finished inventory (days' sales next quarter)	5 days	5 days
Failure rate of finished production	2%	2.5%
Finance and other costs of holding a unit in inventory per quarter	£6.00	£7.00

The failed units are only discovered after completion of the products and they have no resale value.

Other information available is as follows:

Weeks in each quarter	12 weeks
Days per week	5 days
Hours per week	35 hours
Number of employees	70 employees
Budgeted labour rate per hour	£8.00
Overtime premium for hours worked in excess of 35 hours per week	50%
Budgeted cost of material per kg	£10.00
Opening inventory of raw materials	2,800 kgs
Closing inventory of raw materials (days' current quarter's production)	6 days
Financing and other costs of keeping 1 kg of raw material in inventory per quarter	£2.00

Complete the following for quarter 1

- The number of production days are [ ]
- The closing finished inventory of Aye in units is [ ]
- The closing finished inventory of Bee in units is [ ]
- The labour hours available before overtime has to be paid are [ ]
- Production budget (units): Aye [ ]

  Bee [ ]
- Materials purchases budget (kg) [ ]
- Materials purchases budget (£) [ ]
- Labour usage budget (hours) [ ]
- Labour cost budget (£) [ ]
- The cost saving arising from the change in inventory levels for quarter 1 is

£	

Task 4.15

The following sales forecasts are for periods of 20 days (four five-day weeks).

Sales forecast

Sales forecast					
Period number	1	2	3	4	5
Number of Gammas	19,400	21,340	23,280	22,310	22,310

- On completion of production, 3% of units are found to be faulty and have to be scrapped with nil scrap value.
- Opening inventory: period 1
  - Finished inventory 3,880 units
  - Raw materials 16,500 litres
- Closing inventory at the end of each period
  - Finished inventory must equal 4 days' sales volume in the next period.
  - Raw materials must equal 5 days' gross production in the next period.
- Each unit requires 3 litres of material costing £8 per litre.
- Each unit requires 0.5 hours of labour.
- There are 70 production workers who each work a 40 hour week, for which each employee is paid a guaranteed wage of £240 per week.
- The cost of any overtime is £9 per hour.

Prepare the following budgets for Periods 1 to 3 and the gross production budget for Period 4.

		Period 1	Period 2	Period 3	Period 4
(i)	Gross production budget (units)				
(ii)	Materials purchases budget (litres)				
(iii)	Materials purchases budget (£)				
(iv)	Labour budget (hours)				
(v)	Labour budget (£)				

Task 4.16

A company manufactures and sells a single product X. The directors of the company are considering a new low price strategy for the year to 31 December 20X1 which would involve decreasing the price of X by 10%. This is expected to increase volumes by 15%.

The directors had already drawn up a draft operating budget based on their current pricing strategy and wish to revise this budget to see what might happen if the new strategy was adopted.

(a) You are asked to prepare a revised operating budget in the Revision column below and calculate the increase or decrease in profit that would result.

Draft operating budget	Draft	Revision
Sales units	210,000	
	£	£
Sales price	7.00	
Sales revenue	1,470,000	
Variable production costs	924,000	
Fixed production costs	325,000	
Gross profit	221,000	
	▼	

Picklist:

Gross profit will decrease by
Gross profit will increase by

(b) The draft budget for raw materials needed to make product X shows a figure of £427,500. This assumed a 5% decrease in production volume and the same raw material prices as last year.

In actual fact, new information now suggests that production volumes will stay the same but raw materials prices will fall by 10%.

Calculate the material cost forecast:

£	

(c) The draft administration salary budget is £244,800. This originally included the assumption that the annual standard 2% pay rise would apply from 1 January 20X1. However, due to the poor economic outlook the company has decided to decrease wages by 2% instead.

Calculate the revised salary budget:

£	

Task 4.17

Calculate the sales revenue and cost budgets for April using the budgeted unit data and the information below.

- Each unit is made from 3 kg of material costing £0.75 per kg.
- It takes five minutes to make each item.
- 1,250 hours of basic time is available in the month. Any extra hours must be worked in overtime.
- The basic rate is £16 per hour. Overtime is paid at 50% above basic rate.
- Variable overhead relates to labour hours, including overtime.
- Fixed production overhead costs are spread evenly through the year.

Budgeted units	Year	April
Units sold	216,000	18,200
Units produced	210,000	18,000

Budget in £	Year	April
Sales revenue	1,166,400	
Material used	472,500	
Direct labour	300,000	
Variable production overhead	77,000	
Fixed production overhead	13,200	

Task 4.18

A company has constructed the following budgets about the coming month.

Selling price	£6.50 per unit	
Direct materials	2 kg per unit	£0.75 per kg
Direct labour	6 minutes per unit	£12 per hour
Fixed production overheads	£16,000	
Car purchase	£20,000	

Budgeted production is 25,000 units and all units are sold in the month of production. No inventories of material are held.

Complete the following budgeted operating statement and capital budget.

Budgeted operating statement (total absorption basis)

	£	£
Revenue		
Less cost of sales:		
Direct materials		
Direct labour		
Production overheads		
Cost of sales		
Gross profit		

Capital budget

	£
Capital purchase	
Total	

***

Task 4.19

Describe two types of unethical behaviour that can arise from budgeting.

Task 4.20

A business manufactures three bathroom cleaning products: X, Y and Z.

Budget production of product X is 380 units and requires 2.5 machine hours per unit.

Budget production of product Y is 440 units and requires 1 machine hour per unit.

Budget production of product Z is 700 units and requires 0.75 machine hours per unit.

There are four machines in the department. Each machine can be used for 400 hours in the month of September.

Calculate whether or not additional machines must be hired to meet required production in the month of September.

Product	Units	Hours per unit	Hours required
X			
Y			
Z			
Total			
Total machine hours available			

Chapter 5 – Preparing cash budgets

Task 5.1

A business makes 30% of its monthly sales for cash with the remainder being sold on credit. On average 40% of the total sales are received in the month following the sale and the remainder in the second month after the sale. Budgeted sales figures are estimated to be as follows:

	£
August	240,000
September	265,000
October	280,000
November	250,000
December	220,000

Complete the following.

	October	November	December
Budgeted cash receipts from sales (£)			

Task 5.2

A business purchases all of its goods on credit from suppliers. 20% of purchases are offered a discount of 2% for payment in the month of purchase and the business takes advantage of these discounts. A further 45% of purchases are paid for in the month after the purchase and the remainder two months after the purchase. Purchases figures are estimated to be as follows:

	£
August	180,000
September	165,000
October	190,000
November	200,000
December	220,000

Complete the following.

	October	November	December
Budgeted cash payments for purchases (£)			

Task 5.3

A business sells its single product for £50 which produces a gross profit margin of 40%. The product is purchased in the month of sale and is paid for in the month following the purchase.

Estimated sales quantities are as follows:

	Units
July	5,000
August	5,200
September	5,500
October	5,750

Complete the following.

	August	September	October
Cash payments to suppliers (£)			

Task 5.4

Assume no opening and closing inventory.

Forecast annual sales of £6,000 and a mark up of 33⅓%, means forecast purchases of

£	

Forecast annual purchases of £12,000 and a margin of 20%, means forecast sales of

£	

Forecast annual sales of £16,000 and forecast annual profits of £6,000, mean forecast mark-up of [ ] % and margin of [ ] %.

Task 5.5

A business makes all of its sales on credit with a 3% settlement discount offered for payment within the month of the sale. 25% of sales take up this settlement discount and 70% of sales are paid in the following month. The remainder are irrecoverable debts.

Budgeted sales figures are as follows:

	£
March	650,000
April	600,000
May	580,000
June	550,000

Complete the following.

	April	May	June
Budgeted cash receipts for sales (£)			

Task 5.6

A business manufactures and sells a single product, each unit of which requires 20 minutes of labour. The wage rate is £8.40 per hour. The sales of the product are anticipated to be:

	April	May	June	July
Sales units	7,200	7,050	6,550	6,150

The product is produced one month prior to sale and wages are paid in the month of production. Inventory levels of finished goods are to remain at 1,000 units until the end of May when they will be reduced to 900 units and reduced further to 750 units at the end of June.

Complete the following.

	April	May	June
Budgeted cash wages payments (£)			

Task 5.7

Recent actual and estimated sales figures are as follows.

	£
April (actual)	420,000
May (actual)	400,000
June (estimate)	480,000
July (estimate)	500,000
August (estimate)	520,000
September (estimate)	510,000

All sales are on credit and the payment pattern is as follows.

20% pay in the month of sale after taking a 4% settlement discount.

40% pay in the month following the sale.

25% pay two months after the month of sale.

12% pay three months after the month of sale.

There are expected to be 3% irrecoverable debts.

The purchases of the business are all on credit and it is estimated that the following purchases will be made.

	£
May	250,000
June	240,000
July	280,000
August	300,000
September	310,000

40% of purchases are paid for in the month after the purchase has been made and the remainder are paid for two months after the month of purchase.

Wages are expected to be £60,000 each month and are paid in the month in which they are incurred. General overheads are anticipated to be a monthly £50,000 for June and July increasing to £55,000 thereafter. 75% of the general overheads are paid in the month in which they are incurred and the remainder in the following month. The general overheads figure includes a depreciation charge of £6,000 each month.

Selling expenses are expected to be 10% of the monthly sales value and are paid for in the month following the sale.

The business has planned to purchase new equipment for £42,000 in August and in the same month to dispose of old equipment with estimated sales proceeds of £7,500.

Overdraft interest is charged at 1% per month based on the overdraft balance at the start of the month. At 1 July it is anticipated that the business will have an overdraft of £82,000.

Complete the cash budget for July, August and September.

	July £	August £	September £
Opening balance	(82,000)		
Cash receipts:			
Sales			
Proceeds from sale of equipment			
Total receipts			
Cash payments:			
Purchases			
Wages			
Overheads			
Selling expenses			
Equipment			
Overdraft interest			
Total payments			
Closing balance			

Task 5.8

An organisation operates in a highly seasonal sector of the retail industry. The company's management is estimating its cash requirements for the third quarter of the year, for which the following schedule of anticipated inflows and outflows has been produced by the sales and purchases departments.

Month	Sales £	Purchases £
May	160,000	240,000
June	320,000	60,000
July	80,000	40,000
August	80,000	120,000
September	160,000	180,000
October	220,000	120,000
November	180,000	80,000

Sales are made on two months' credit, whilst suppliers allow one month's credit. Monthly salaries amount to £36,000 and the company's annual rent of £48,000 is paid quarterly in advance.

An overdraft of £112,000 is expected to exist on 30 June.

Complete the cash budget for July, August and September.

	July £000	August £000	September £000
Opening balance	(112)		
Cash receipts:			
Sales			
Cash payments:			
Purchases			
Salaries			
Rent			
Total payments			
Closing balance			

Task 5.9

A manufacturing business is to prepare its cash budget for the three months ending 31 December. The business manufactures a single product which requires 3 kg of raw material per unit and 3 hours of labour per unit. Production takes place in the month of sale. The raw material cost is anticipated to be £9 per kg and the labour force are paid at a rate of £7.20 per hour. Each unit of the product sells for £75.

The forecast sales in units are as follows.

	August	September	October	November	December
Forecast sales – units	5,000	5,100	5,400	5,800	6,000

Sales are on credit with 40% of receivables paying the month after sale and the remainder two months after the sale.

Inventory of completed units is anticipated to be 500 until the start of October but this is to be increased by 100 units each month at the end of October, November and December.

The raw materials required for production are purchased in the month prior to production and 60% are paid for in the following month and the remainder two months after purchase. The anticipated inventory of raw materials is 3,000 kgs until the end of September and the planned inventory levels at the end of each month thereafter are as follows:

October	3,200 kgs
November	3,500 kgs
December	4,000 kgs

Wages are paid in the month in which they are incurred.

Production overheads are expected to be £60,000 each month and are paid for in the month in which they are incurred. This figure includes depreciation of £10,000 per month for machinery. General overheads are anticipated to be £72,000 each month in October and November increasing to £80,000 in December and are paid in the month in which they are incurred. The figure for general overheads includes £12,000 of depreciation each month.

The cash balance at 1 October is expected to be £40,000 in credit.

Complete the cash budget for October, November and December.

	October £	November £	December £
Opening balance	40,000		
Cash receipts:			
Sales			
Cash payments:			
Purchases			
Wages			
Production overheads			
General overheads			
Total payments			
Net cash flow for the month			
Closing balance			

Task 5.10

A manufacturing business has the following extracts from its budgeted statement of financial position and its budgeted income statement for the following year 20X5, along with the actual balances and results for 20X4.

Statement of financial position

	As at 31 December 20X4 £	As at 31 December 20X5 £
Receivables	23,000	19,000
Payables	5,600	12,800

The payables relate only to supplies of materials.

Income statement

	Y/e 31 December 20X4 £	Y/e 31 December 20X5 £
Sales	240,300	228,400
Materials purchases	120,000	128,000

Calculate the cash flows in respect of sales

£	

Calculate the cash flows in respect of purchases

£	

Chapter 6 – Budget preparation – limiting factors

Task 6.1

A business has budgeted sales demand of 12,000 units in the coming month.

Each unit requires 2 kg of material.

Each unit requires 0.5 machine hours.

Each unit requires 1.5 labour hours.

The availability of resource for the coming period is as follows:

Raw material available = 25,000 kg

There are 5 machines each capable of operating for 1,000 hours.

There are 40 workers each capable of operating for 500 hours.

No inventory of finished goods or raw materials is kept.

What is the limiting factor in the budget?

Select from:

	✓
Sales demand	
Material	
Machine hours	
Labour hours	

Task 6.2

A business makes a single product, each unit of which requires 5 kgs of raw material. Unfortunately, due to a shortage of suppliers of the raw material, only 129,000 kgs will be available in the coming year. The materials are available on a monthly basis spread evenly over the year.

Complete the following.

The number of units that can be produced in total is [ ].

The number of units that can be produced each month is [ ].

Task 6.3

The raw materials requirements for production for the next six months for a business are as follows:

	July	Aug	Sept	Oct	Nov	Dec
Raw materials requirements – kg	4,800	4,300	4,100	4,900	4,200	5,000

It is only possible to purchase 4,500 kg of the product each month.

Complete the following to show the maximum shortage of raw materials in kgs over the six-month period, monthly and in total, if only the amount required (up to the maximum allowed) is purchased each month.

Purchasing plan 1:

	July	Aug	Sept	Oct	Nov	Dec
Requirement						
Purchase						
Shortage						

Total shortage: [ ] kgs

Complete the following to show how many kgs of the material should be purchased each month in order to maximise production and keep inventory levels to the minimum possible. Give the total shortage of raw materials over the six-month period under this policy.

Purchasing plan 2:

	July	Aug	Sept	Oct	Nov	Dec
Requirement						
Purchase						
Excess/(Shortage)						
Inventory						
Production						

Total shortage: [ ] kgs

Task 6.4

Explain how a business could try to alleviate the problem of shortage of materials if:

(a) The shortage is a short-term problem and full supplies will be available after a few months; or

(b) The shortage is a long-term problem?

Task 6.5

The raw materials requirements for production for Selby Electronics for the next six months are as follows:

	May	June	July	Aug	Sep	Oct
Raw materials requirements – kg	9,500	10,200	10,200	9,300	10,200	10,300

Selby is only able to purchase 10,000 kgs of the material in each month.

Complete the following which schedules the purchases in order to ensure the maximum production over the six-month period together with the minimum possible inventory level. Give the level of shortage under this purchasing plan.

Purchasing plan:

	May	June	July	Aug	Sep	Oct
Material requirement						
Potential shortage						
Purchases						
Inventory						
Production						

Total shortage: [ ] kgs

Task 6.6

A product requires three hours of skilled labour per unit but there are only 12 such employees. They normally work a 38-hour week although, by paying an overtime rate of double time, it has been possible to negotiate for each employee to work eight hours of overtime a week.

The maximum level of production each week is [ ] units.

Describe other ways of solving the labour shortage problem.

Task 6.7

Next week sales demand is expected to be 1,860 units. Each unit requires four hours of direct labour time and there are 160 employees each working a 35 hour week.

What is the overtime (in hours) required in order to meet demand with the current workforce?

Select from:

	✓
1,840	
3,740	
7,440	
5,600	

Task 6.8

There are two identical production lines in a factory. The factory operates two seven-hour shifts each day for five days a week with the production lines working at full capacity. The production line is capable of producing 30 units of product per hour.

The maximum production for a week is [ ] units.

State the options that should be considered if sales demand were to exceed the maximum production level.

Task 6.9

Give three examples of possible key budget factors for a manufacturing organisation other than sales demand.

Task 6.10

In each of the following situations, suggest what may be the key budget factor:

	Key budget factor
A private nursing home with 140 beds. The home is situated in an area which has a large proportion of retired people amongst the population and there is little difficulty in recruiting suitable staff.	
A vendor of ice cream in a busy shopping centre. The transportable stall can store a maximum of 50 litres of ice cream.	
A partnership of three skilled craftsmen making carved chess sets from wood and marble for home sales and exports to specific order. Sales demand is high and orders have to be frequently rejected.	
A manufacturer of home cinema sound systems which are similar to those of other manufacturers and who distributes the systems amongst a number of small high street electrical retailers.	

Task 6.11

Four products have the following sales price and resource requirements.

	W	X	Y	Z
Sales price £	200	90	180	150
Materials (kg)	20	8	19	12
Labour (hours)	4	5	12	6
Maximum demand	300	1500	400	1000

The material costs £3 per kg.

Cost of labour is £6 per hour.

Materials are restricted to 20,000 kg.

Complete the production schedule.

	Production units
Product W	
Product X	
Product Y	
Product Z	

Chapter 7 – Budgetary control – comparing budget and actual costs

Task 7.1

The budget for production supervisors' costs for a period at an activity level of 250,000 units is £15,000. One production supervisor is required for every 100,000 units of production.

If actual production is 330,000 units, what figure would appear in the flexed budget for production supervisors' costs?

Select from:

	✓
£60,000	
£20,000	
£15,000	
£19,800	

Task 7.2

Activity level	100,000 units	120,000 units
	£	£
Materials cost	240,000	288,000
Labour cost	124,000	144,000
Production overhead	38,000	38,000

The costs which would appear in a budget flexed to an actual activity level of 112,000 units would be:

Material cost

£	

Labour cost

£	

Production overhead

£	

Task 7.3

The budgeted production overhead for a business is £524,000 at an activity level of 60,000 units and £664,000 at an activity level of 80,000 units.

If the actual activity level is 72,000 units, the flexed budget figure for production overhead is:

£	

Task 7.4

Complete the following flexed budget, given the following details of the cost behaviour of each of the costs.

Materials	The materials cost is totally variable
Labour	Each operative can only produce 2,000 units each quarter – the cost of each operative is £3,500 each quarter
Production overhead	The production overhead is a totally fixed cost
General expenses	The general expenses are made up of a budgeted fixed cost of £6,400 and a variable element

Actual sales and production were in fact only 15,000 units during quarter 4. Prepare a flexed budget for an activity level of 15,000 units.

	Budget 20,000 units £	Flexed budget 15,000 units £
Sales (20,000 units)	130,000	
Material	(55,000)	
Labour	(35,000)	
Production overhead	(18,000)	
Gross profit	22,000	
General expenses	12,000	
Operating profit	10,000	

Task 7.5

Given below is the original fixed budget for a manufacturing operation for quarter 2. However, as sales and production were subsequently anticipated to be higher than this budget made allowance for, a revised budget was also prepared. The actual results for quarter 2 are also given.

	Original budget 200,000 units		Revised budget 240,000 units		Actual 230,000 units	
	£	£	£	£	£	£
Sales		1,360,000		1,632,000		1,532,000
Materials	690,000		828,000		783,200	
Labour	387,000		449,000		428,600	
Production						
Expenses	162,000		186,000		173,500	
Production cost		1,239,000		1,463,000		1,385,300
Gross profit		121,000		169,000		146,700
General						
Expenses		72,000		72,000		74,700
Operating profit		49,000		97,000		72,000

Complete the following flexed budget to reflect the actual level of activity for the quarter, and calculate the variances from that budget.

	Flexed budget units		Actual units		Variances
	£	£	£	£	£
Sales				1,532,000	
Materials			783,200		
Labour			428,600		
Production expenses			173,500		
Production cost				1,385,300	
Gross profit				146,700	
General expenses				74,700	
Operating profit				72,000	

Task 7.6

Given below is the budget for quarter 2 prepared using absorption costing principles. There was no opening inventory.

	Quarter 2 budget	
	£	£
Sales (50,000 units)		400,000
Materials	165,400	
Labour	69,800	
Production overhead	56,000	
Cost of production		
56,000 units	291,200	
Less: closing inventory	31,200	
Cost of sales		260,000
Gross profit		140,000
General expenses		52,000
Operating profit		88,000

The materials and labour costs are variable with the level of production but the production overhead and general expenses are both fixed costs.

Complete the following budget for quarter 2 using marginal costing principles, and reconcile the budgeted profit figure using absorption costing to the budgeted profit figure using marginal costing.

	£	£
Sales 50,000 units		
Materials		
Labour		
Cost of production: 56,000 units		
Less: closing inventory		
Cost of sales		
Contribution		
Production overhead		
General expenses		
Operating profit		

	£
Profit per absorption costing budget	88,000
▼	
Profit per marginal costing budget	

Picklist:

General expenses included in closing inventory
Production overhead included in closing inventory
Production overhead included in opening inventory

Task 7.7

A business has supplied you with the following information.

	£	Kg
Favourable material price variance	1,370	
Actual kg purchased		6,850
Actual cost of materials	21,920	

Complete the following sentence.

The standard material price is £ [ ] per kg (to 2 dp)

Task 7.8

A business has supplied you with the following information.

	£	Hours
Favourable material price variance	150	
Standard cost per kilogram of material	15	
Actual cost of material	615	
Adverse labour rate variance	360	
Actual labour hours		575
Actual cost of labour	7,835	

Complete the following two sentences.

The actual quantity of material used is [ ] kg.

The standard labour rate is £ [ ] per hour

Task 7.9

A business's sales director unexpectedly resigns during the year.

What effect might this have on variances?

Task 7.10

Due to the sudden illness of the credit controller, the credit control function is outsourced to an external agency during the year.

What effect might this have on variances?

Task 7.11

Why is it important that managerial performance is only judged on the basis of controllable variances?

Task 7.12

Given below is the original fixed budget and the actual results for the same period.

	Budget		Actual	
Units	30,000		34,000	
	£	£	£	£
Sales		660,000		697,000
Direct costs				
Materials	252,000		299,200	
Labour	180,000		192,600	
Factory power	83,600		88,600	
	515,600		580,400	
Fixed overheads	75,000		79,000	
Cost of sales		590,600		659,400
Operating profit		69,400		37,600

You are also provided with the following information:

(i) There is no inventory of finished goods

(ii) The production employees are paid per week irrespective of the production level. The employees that were budgeted for are capable of producing a maximum of 45,000 units in a six-month period

(iii) The budgeted and actual figures for factory power include a fixed cost element of £20,600

Prepare a report for the Chief Executive including the following:

A flexed operating statement for the actual activity level using marginal costing principles, calculating the variances for the sales and costs figures, as set out below.

An explanation of why the flexed budget operating statement shows different results from that of the original budget.

Units	Flexed budget 34,000		Actual 34,000		Variance A/F
	£	£	£	£	£
Sales					
Direct costs					
Materials					
Factory power					
Subtotal					
Contribution					
Labour					
Factory power					
Fixed overheads					
Fixed costs					
Operating profit					

Task 7.13

A business makes a car stereo that is fitted to the cars made by its parent company

You have the following information.

- Two draft budgets for the coming year. The first assumes a production and sales volume of 80,000 car stereos. The second assumes a production and sales volume of 100,000 car stereos. Any differences between the two budgets arose entirely from the different volumes assumed.
- The actual operating results for the year.
- A note stating there was no opening or closing inventory of any sort.
- A note stating that there were no purchases or sales of non-current assets during the year.

The draft budgets and actual results from the working papers are shown below.

Budgets and actual results

	Draft budgets				Actual results	
Car stereo production and sales volume	80,000		100,000		140,000	
	£000	£000	£000	£000	£000	£000
Conversion costs						
Labour	640		760		972	
Light, heat and power	370		450		586	
Rent, rates and insurance	200		200		200	
Depreciation	150		150		132	
		1,360		1,560		1,890
Bought-in materials		1,600		2,000		3,220
Total expense		2,960		3,560		5,110
Sales revenue		3,200		4,000		6,440
Operating profit		240		440		1,330

Complete the following flexed budget statement showing the budgeted and actual results and any variances.

	Flexed budget	Actual results	Variances A/F	Variances A/F
Production and sales volume (Car stereos)	140,000	140,000		
	£000	£000	£000	%
Conversion costs				
Labour		972		
Light, heat and power		586		
Rent, rates and insurance		200		
Depreciation		132		
Total conversion costs		1,890		
Bought-in materials		3,220		
Total expenses		5,110		
Sales revenue		6,440		
Operating profit		1,330		

The Chief Executive believes the high profits of £1,330,000 are due to increased effort by the managers following the introduction of performance related pay at the beginning of this year. Details of the scheme are:

- The bought-in materials for the car stereos are purchased from outside suppliers but the conversion costs – those manufacturing costs that transform the raw materials into the finished product – are all provided the company.
- The only customer for the car stereo is the parent company. Because of this, there is no market price and so the price has had to be negotiated.
- It was agreed that the price of the car stereos sold to the parent company should be twice the cost of the bought-in materials.
- Additional performance related payments are based on the following:
  - Exceeding the annual budgeted volume of sales
  - Increasing the actual profit per car stereo above the budgeted profit per cr stereo

- The budgeted sales volume for the year was 100,000 car stereos and the budgeted profit per car stereo was £4.40.
- The actual sales volume for the year was 140,000 and the actual profit per car stereo was £9.50.

Write a memo to the Chief Executive, which covers the following:

Use the data in the question to explain three reasons why profits might have improved even without the introduction of performance related pay.

Identify three general conditions necessary for performance related pay to lead to improved performance.

Task 7.14

Given below are key variances for the month of November, calculated using the flexed budget.

Key variances – November

	Variances	
	Adverse £	Favourable £
Materials	23,700	
Labour		2,200
Fixed overhead	7,200	

You also discover the following information:

- Due to staff shortages a more junior grade of labour than normal from one of the other factories had to be used in the production process, giving rise to inefficiencies and additional wastage.
- The materials price has been increased by all suppliers and it is doubtful that the materials can be purchased more cheaply than this in future.
- Due to its inventory-holding policy, the factory has had to rent some additional space but this has not been recognised in the standard fixed overhead cost.
- Due to the inefficiencies of labour, more hours had to be worked than normal in the month.

Write a report to the Managing Director, explaining the possible reasons for the variances for the month and making any suggestions about future actions that should be taken.

Task 7.15

You have been provided with the following operating statement for Soupzz Ltd which produces vegetable soup using mainly carrots and potatoes.

Variances	Favourable	Adverse
Direct materials (carrots) price		£1,750
Direct materials (carrots) usage	£760	
Direct materials (potatoes) price	£450	
Direct materials (potatoes) usage		£1,700

The chef has given you the following information about the ingredients and production of the soup:

- The region where Soupzz's carrot supplier is located has recently been hit by flooding which means that much of the carrot crop was destroyed. Soupzz Ltd has had to use suppliers from further afield to get the required quantity of carrots. One of these new suppliers has provided some very sweet tasting carrots with a stronger flavour and Soupzz Ltd is considering whether to change suppliers next year.

- Soupzz has very little control over the price it pays for its carrots as this is dependent on the quantity and the quality of carrots produced – which is influenced by the weather.

  Following some bad press about carbohydrates making people fat, general demand for potatoes has dropped and this has led to potato suppliers reducing their prices. As the carrots were sweeter, Soupzz used more potatoes and fewer carrots in its soup than usual.

- There was a fault in one of the machines which took a long time to be fixed. This resulted in labour staff temporarily having nothing to do.

Using this information, prepare a report to the Production Director to cover the following:

(a) Provide possible reasons for the carrots and potatoes variances by considering the following:

- Price of the ingredients
- Quality of the ingredients
- Mix of ingredients

(b) Discuss the type of labour variance that the machine breakdown would have caused.

To:
From:

Subject:
Date:

(a) Possible reasons for the variances

- Direct materials (carrots) price variance

- Direct materials (carrots) usage variance

- Direct materials (potatoes) price variance

- Direct materials (potatoes) usage variance

(b) Machine downtime and labour variances

Chapter 8 – Performance indicators in budgetary control

Task 8.1

Suggest suitable non-financial performance indicators to compare budgeted versus actual performance for an online clothes shop.

Task 8.2

Suggest possible measures of productivity for each of the following types of organisation:

- A vet's surgery
- A bar
- A firm of solicitors
- A retail store
- A wedding cake business

Task 8.3

A component is made by the manual operation of a number of cutting machines. The process produces shavings of material which are collected each day, and stored until removed by a rubbish collection service.

What performance measures or indicators will be useful to the production manager with regard to material?

Task 8.4

At an accountancy firm, trainees spend part of their time at college, and part in the office.

What performance measures will be useful for the Office Managing Partner in relation to trainees?

Task 8.5

A business uses a small number of large machines, which are only replaced every 20 years.

Suggest useful performance measures relating to the machines.

Task 8.6

Suggest performance indicators to measure customer service by a restaurant.

Task 8.7

A bus company collects the following information in order to monitor performance.

- Number of drivers
- Number of passengers
- Number of miles travelled
- Number of journeys undertaken
- Maintenance costs

This information is known over any time period.

Suggest measures that could be used to compare budgeted and actual performance in order to monitor the following performance indicators:

- Driver productivity
- Satisfaction of passenger needs indicators, using the information collected
- Satisfaction of passenger needs indicators, which would require other information
- Safety indicators, using existing information
- Safety indicators, requiring other information

Task 8.8

Billy runs a gardening business called Great Growers.

His financial data for the last two years is as follows:

	20X7	20X8
Sales	120,000	160,000
Materials	13,000	17,000
Labour costs	40,000	55,000
Gross profit	67,000	88,000

Other information:

Billy expects to visit a client on average 4 times a year.

In 20X7 there were two members of staff employed. One new staff member joined at the start of 20X8. There were no increases in pay for existing staff in 20X8.

The number of complaints that Billy received in 20X7 was 12 and in 20X8 this was 26.

The number of customers who requested Billy's services 4 times during the year in 20X7 was 425, in 20X8 this number was 420.

Total customers in 20X7 were 480 and in 20X8 total customers were 650.

Calculate two appropriate quality measures.

Task 8.9

Using your answers from Task 8.8 and the information provided in the task, comment on how the quality of service has changed and suggest why this may have happened.

Task 8.10

You are given the following information for the production department of M Ltd.

Production units	500,000
Machine hours per unit	0.25
Machine hours needed	125,000
Machine hours available	150,000
Machine maintenance cost	£30,000
Production cost	£2,500,000

Suggest appropriate performance indicators for this department

Answer Bank

Chapter 1

Task 1.1

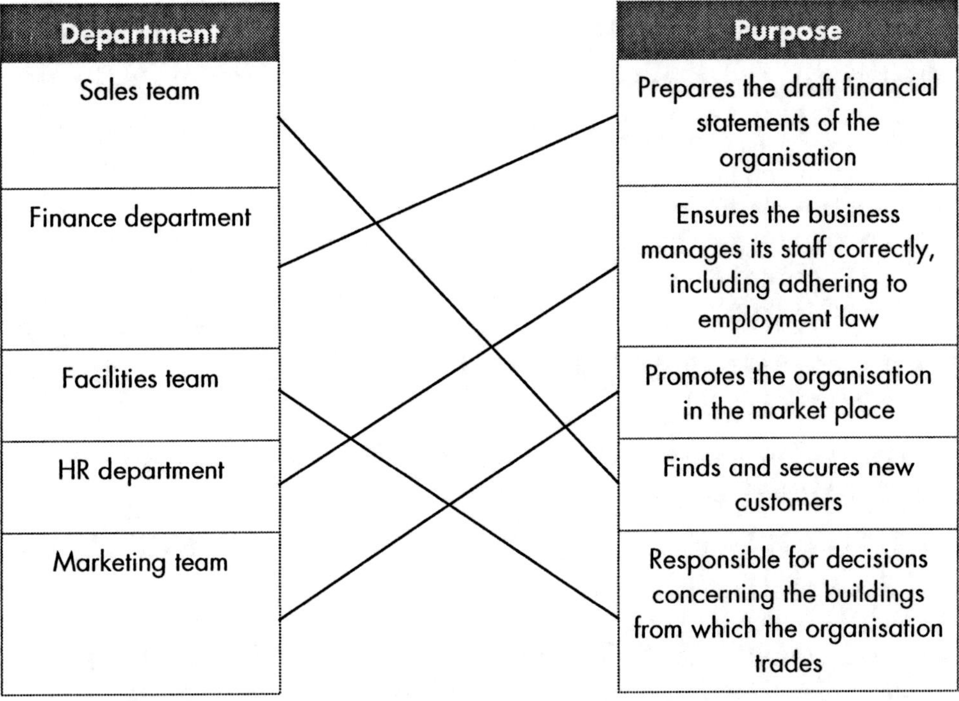

Task 1.2

Cost	Budget
Market research survey	Marketing budget
Wages of factory workers	Production budget
Recruitment advertisement for a new finance director in an accountancy magazine	Administrative overheads budget
Raw material costs	Production budget
Salary of marketing director	Marketing budget

Task 1.3

Function	Department
Prepares accounting information, pays suppliers and staff, chases customers for payment etc	Finance department
Recruits, develops and disciplines staff, and ensures that employment law is followed by the business	HR department
Buys raw materials for use in the production process	Purchasing team
Makes sales to new and existing customers	Sales team
Investigates and responds to customer complaints	After-sales service team

Task 1.4

Costs	Responsibility centre
Client entertaining at horse racing	Marketing department
Repair of security alarm system in offices	Administration department
Sick pay for production manager	Production department
Bonus for sales managers	Sales team
Depreciation of production equipment	Production department

Task 1.5

Cost	Behaviour
Room hire	Fixed
Food for attendees	Variable
Hire of waiting staff – 1 required per 20 attendees	Stepped

Task 1.6

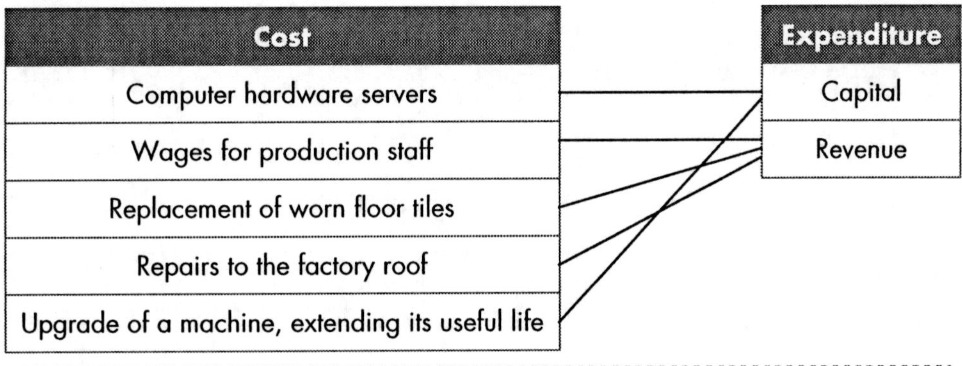

Task 1.7

True ☑

False ☐

Workings

	20,000 units	32,000 units
Total cost	£128,000	£204,800
Cost per unit	£6.40	£6.40

Therefore this is a variable cost as cost per unit is the same at each activity level.

Task 1.8

Cost	Apportionment basis
Heating	Floor area
Rental on storage unit for raw materials	Average inventory of raw materials
Canteen expenses	Number of staff employed
Depreciation of factory building	Floor area

Task 1.9

	Cost behaviour
Cost 1	Fixed
Cost 2	Stepped
Cost 3	Variable
Cost 4	Semi-variable

Task 1.10

Activity level (units)	Budgeted total production cost £	Budgeted cost per unit £
8,000	33,400	4.18
12,000	42,600	3.55
15,000	49,500	3.30

Workings

	8,000 units	12,000 units	15,000 units
	£	£	£
Variable costs			
£23,000/10,000 × 8,000	18,400		
£23,000/10,000 × 12,000		27,600	
£23,000/10,000 × 15,000			34,500
Fixed costs	15,000	15,000	15,000
	33,400	42,600	49,500
Cost per unit	£4.18	£3.55	£3.30

Task 1.11

	Cost behaviour
Maintenance contract which costs £10,000 annually plus an average of £500 cost per call out	Semi-variable
Sales car depreciation based upon miles travelled	Variable
Machine consumables cost based on machine hours	Variable
Rent for a building that houses the factory, stores and maintenance departments	Fixed

Task 1.12

Costs	Accounting treatment
Servicing of office computer equipment	Allocate to administrative overheads
Materials wastage in production process	Direct cost
Depreciation of marketing director's car	Allocate to marketing overheads
Bonus for finance director	Allocate to administrative overheads
Sick pay for production workers	Charge to production in a labour hour overhead rate

Task 1.13

(i) Absorption costing

£	67.69

(ii) Marginal costing

£	61.46

Workings

(i) Absorption costing

Apportionment of overheads

	Cutting £	Finishing £	Stores £
Allocated overhead	380,000	280,000	120,000
Stores overhead apportioned 80:20	96,000	24,000	(120,000)
	476,000	304,000	–
Hours worked 50,000 × 3	150,000		
50,000 × 2		100,000	
Overhead absorption rate	476,000	304,000	
	150,000	100,000	
	= £3.17 per	= £3.04 per	
	labour hour	labour hour	

Unit cost – absorption costing

		£
Direct materials		16.00
Labour –	cutting 3 hours × £7.50	22.50
	finishing 2 hours × £6.80	13.60
Overheads –	cutting 3 hours × £3.17	9.51
	finishing 2 hours × £3.04	6.08
Unit cost		67.69

(ii) Marginal costing

Unit cost – marginal costing

	£
Direct materials	16.00
Labour – cutting 3 hours × £7.50	22.50
finishing 2 hours × £6.80	13.60
Cutting £380,000 × 60%/50,000	4.56
Finishing £280,000 × 60%/50,000	3.36
Stores £120,000 × 60%/50,000	1.44
Unit cost	61.46

Task 1.14

File note

To: Drampton's finance director
From: Financial analyst
Date: xx.xx.xx
Subject: **Little Ltd – treatment of fixed overheads**

Introduction

Following our recent discussions, I set out below calculations showing the reclassification of fixed overheads between the two units manufactured by Little Ltd, using activity-based costing.

	Allocated overheads to Server £	Allocated overheads to PC £
Set-up costs	10,000	–
Rent and power (production area)	24,000	96,000
Rent (stores area)	25,000	25,000
Salaries of store issue staff	8,000	32,000

Step 1. Calculation of cost per cost driver

	Budgeted total annual overheads £	Cost driver	Number of cost drivers	Cost per cost driver £
Set-up costs	10,000	Number of set-ups	5	2,000.00
Rent and power(production area)	120,000	Number of wks' production	50	2,400.00
Rent (stores area)	50,000	Floor area of stores (m2)	800	62.50
Salaries of store issue staff	40,000	No of issues of inventory	10,000	4.00
	220,000			

Step 2. Reallocation of overheads based on costs per cost driver

Server	(i) Number of cost drivers	(ii) Cost per cost driver £	(i) × (ii) Allocated overheads
Set-up costs	5	2,000.00	10,000
Rent & power (production area)	10	2,400.00	24,000
Rent (stores area)	400	62.50	25,000
Salaries of store issue staff	2,000	4.00	8,000
			67,000

PC	(i) Number of cost drivers	(ii) Cost per cost driver £	(i) × (ii) Allocated overheads
Set-up costs	0	2,000.00	–
Rent & power (production area)	40	2,400.00	96,000
Rent (stores area)	400	62.50	25,000
Salaries of store issue staff	8,000	4.00	32,000
			153,000

Chapter 2

Task 2.1

Data
The previous year's financial statements for a competitor company
Previous month's discounts allowed
Industry average profit margin
Information about a competitor's success
Average sick days of employees per month

Source
Financial press
Companies House
HR department
Trade association
Internal accounting records

Task 2.2

	✓
Forecast labour hours per unit and labour cost per hour	
Forecast production units and labour cost per unit	✓
Forecast sales units and labour hours per unit	
Forecast production units and labour hours per unit	

The labour usage budget requires the forecast production units and labour hours per unit.

Task 2.3

	✓
Production budget	
Opening and closing inventory of finished goods	
Sales budget	
Opening and closing inventory of raw materials	✓

If the materials usage budget is already known, this will have already taken account of inventory of finished goods, and the production budget.

Task 2.4

The general limitations of forecasting are:

- The less historical data that is used, the more unreliable the results of the forecast will be.
- The further into the future that the forecast considers, the more unreliable it will become.
- Forecast figures will often be based upon the assumption that current conditions will continue in the future. A trend of results may be based upon historical data, but you cannot always assume that the trend will continue in the future.
- If the forecast is based upon a trend, there are always random elements or variations which cause the trend to change.
- The forecast produced from the historical data may be quite accurate but the actual future results may be very different from the forecast figures due to changes in the political, economic or technological environment within which the business operates.

Task 2.5

Quarter	Forecast sales (units)
Quarter 2	112,060
Quarter 3	136,262
Quarter 4	118,611

Workings

	Trend	Seasonal variation		Forecast
Quarter 2 ((122,000 – 6,000) × 1.035)	120,060	–8,000	=	112,060
Quarter 3 (120,060 × 1.035)	124,262	+12,000	=	136,262
Quarter 4 (124,262 × 1.035)	128,611	–10,000	=	118,611

Task 2.6

Quarter	Forecast sales (units)
Quarter 1	278,800
Quarter 2	417,450
Quarter 3	374,500
Quarter 4	319,500

Workings

	Trend	Seasonal variation		Forecast
Quarter 1 (Trend = 335,000 + 5,000)	340,000	× 0.82	=	278,800
Quarter 2	345,000	× 1.21	=	417,450
Quarter 3	350,000	× 1.07	=	374,500
Quarter 4	355,000	× 0.90	=	319,500

Task 2.7

The main limitations of using time series analysis for forecasting are:

- Unless the data used covers many years, it is impossible to isolate the cyclical changes due to general changes in the economy.
- The seasonal variations are an average of the seasonal variation for each period and again, unless this is based on a large amount of historical data, the figure could be misleading.
- Any random variations are ignored.
- The trend and the seasonal variations are assumed to continue in the future in the same manner as in the past.
- If the time series analysis is based upon historic values, the figures will include past inflation which may not be an indication of the future amounts.

Task 2.8

(a) The product life cycle is generally thought to split into five separate stages:

- Development
- Launch
- Growth
- Maturity
- Decline

During the development and launch stage of the product's life there are large outgoings in terms of development expenditure, non-current assets necessary for production, the building up of inventory levels and advertising and promotion expenses. It is likely that even after the launch sales will be quite low and the product will be making a loss at this stage.

If the launch of the product is successful then during the growth stage there will be fairly rapid increases in sales and a move to profitability as the costs of the earlier stages are covered. However, these sales increases are not likely to continue indefinitely.

In the maturity stage of the product, demand for the product will probably start to slow down and become more constant. In many cases this is the stage where the product is modified or improved in order to sustain demand and this may then see a small surge in sales.

At some point in a product's life, unless it is a consumable item such as chocolate bars, the product will reach the end of its sale life, which is known as the decline stage. The market will have bought enough of the product and sales will decline. This is the point where the business should consider no longer producing the product.

(b) If the future demand for a product is to be forecast using time series analysis it is obviously important that the stage in the product life cycle that has been reached is taken into account. For example, if the trend is based upon the growth stage, whereas in fact the product is moving into the maturity stage, then the trend would show an overly optimistic forecast for sales.

Task 2.9

	✓
Development	
Launch	
Growth	
Maturity	✓
Decline	

During the maturity stage the pattern of sales is likely to be more constant.

Task 2.10

	Jan	Feb	Mar	Apr	May	Jun
Forecast variable production costs £ (production units × £10.50)	37,800	30,450	33,600	32,550	35,700	42,000
Forecast variable selling costs £ (sales units × £3.80)	13,300	11,400	11,400	12,160	13,300	14,440

Task 2.11

	Quarter 1	Quarter 2
Forecast direct materials costs £	667,396	722,633

Workings

Quarter 1 £657,000 × 128.4/126.4 = £667,396
Quarter 2 £692,500 × 131.9/126.4 = £722,633

Task 2.12

	Jan	Feb	Mar
Forecast variable production costs £	106,631	113,092	116,161
Forecast variable selling costs £	33,033	35,012	38,047

Working

Variable production costs

		£
January	4,200 × £25 × 137.3/135.2	106,631
February	4,400 × £25 × 139.0/135.2	113,092
March	4,500 × £25 × 139.6/135.2	116,161

Variable selling costs

January	4,100 × £8 × 141.5/140.5	33,033
February	4,300 × £8 × 143.0/140.5	35,012
March	4,650 × £8 × 143.7/140.5	38,047

Task 2.13

The forecast total electricity, machinery maintenance and water costs for the coming month are

£	96,359

Working

		£
Electricity	£35,000 × 95% × 240.3/224.6	35,574
Maintenance costs	£20,000/4 × 2 × 1.05	10,500
Water costs	(£62,000 – 15,000) × 240.3/224.6	50,285
Total		96,359

Task 2.14

The forecast fixed costs for next year are

£	172,320

Working

		£
Rent	£65,000 × 1.055	68,575
Insurance	£15,700 × 1.10	17,270
Power	£84,000 × 171.2/166.3	86,475
		172,320

Task 2.15

The estimated variable cost per machine hour is

£	15

Working

	Machine hours	Cost £
June (lowest)	14,200	285,000
August (highest)	15,200	300,000
Increase	1,000	15,000

Variable cost = £15,000/1,000 hours
= £15 per hour

The estimated fixed costs of the maintenance department are

£	72,000

Working

	£
June	
Variable element £15 × 14,200 hours	213,000
Fixed element (bal fig)	72,000
Total cost	285,000

Task 2.16

Forecast units	Production costs £
74,000	685,000
90,000	797,000

Workings

	Activity level	Cost £
July (lowest)	63,000	608,000
September (highest)	76,000	699,000
Increase	13,000	91,000

Variable element = £91,000/13,000
= £7 per unit

	£
July	
Variable element £7 × 63,000 units	441,000
Fixed element (bal fig)	167,000
Total cost	608,000

Production level of 74,000 units:

	£
Variable cost £7 × 74,000	518,000
Fixed cost	167,000
Total cost	685,000
Production level of 90,000 units:	

	£
Variable cost £7 × 90,000	630,000
Fixed cost	167,000
Total cost	797,000

The estimate for the 74,000 units of production is likely to be more accurate than the estimate for 90,000 units. Estimating the costs at 74,000 units is an example of interpolation, in that the estimate is being made for a production level that is within the range of production levels used to estimate the variable and fixed costs. 90,000 units of production is significantly higher than the levels of production used in estimating fixed and variable costs and therefore it is possible that the costs would behave differently at this level of production. This is an example of extrapolation.

Task 2.17

(i) **Random sampling** means that members of the population have equal chances of being selected. This means that random sampling is completely free from bias in terms of the items included in the sample. The entire population must be known and each item of the population is assigned a sequential number. The items to be sampled are then chosen using random number tables or a random number generator.

In order for random sampling to be used, every item of the population must be known and numbered. For example, this could be used if a check were to be made on the accuracy of calculations on sales invoices for the quarter from January to March. Each sales invoice has a sequential number therefore the first invoice sent out in January would be assigned the number 01, the second invoice sent out 02 etc. The invoices to be checked would then be chosen by random numbers.

(ii) **Stratified sampling** can be used where the population is split into a number of different groups. The size of the population in each group is determined and the size of sample from each group is then based upon the proportionate size of the group to the whole population.

For example, suppose that the sales invoices to be checked for accuracy had been prepared by three different divisions of the company. The number of invoices sent out in the quarter by each division would determine the relative sizes of the samples taken from each division. Once the sizes of the divisional sample were determined, they would each then be chosen using random or systematic sampling.

Chapter 3

Task 3.1

A budget is a formalised, numerical plan of action for all areas of a business for the forthcoming period, normally set for the next twelve-month period.

A budgetary control system can help management to perform their duties in two main areas.

One of the roles of management is in terms of planning for the business – both long term strategic plans and shorter term operational plans. Budgets are formal, numerical plans which can help to ensure that all areas of the business are aiming at the same goals.

For example, once the sales and manufacturing budgets are set, management can then ensure that the budgets for other areas of the business such as the canteen and the sales department are in line with these budgets. So, for example, if it is budgeted that there will be 200 factory workers each day then the canteen should not be budgeting to buy food for 400. Or if sales are expected to be 60,000 units in the period it is important that the sales department budgets in order to be able to deal with this level.

A further important role of management is that of control of operations and of costs in particular. A budgetary system can assist in this area as the eventual actual results can be compared to the budgeted figures and any variances can be calculated and investigated. Where necessary management can then take corrective action to deal with these variances from planned costs.

Task 3.2

Scenario	Budget use
In order to meet a profit target, the managing director reduces the figure in next year's budget for the staff Christmas party by 25%	Cost control
The sales director divides the costs for client entertainment between his two sales teams, and gives the managers of those teams permission to spend within that level	Authorisation
A retail company is wishing to expand its operations and so includes the rental costs of new shops in its budget	Planning
The purchasing manager informs the production manager there will be a world-wide shortage of one type of material in the coming period. The production manager budgets for a different product mix because of this.	Co-ordination

Task 3.3

Budget manual

The budget manual is a set of detailed instructions as to how the budget is to be prepared. The budget manual might typically include the following:

- The names of the budget holders – those responsible for producing each budget
- To whom each budget holder reports
- An organisation chart
- The timescale for the production of each budget
- The procedures for preparing each budget
- The format of the budgets
- How and when actual performance is compared to budget

Budget committee

The budget committee is responsible for co-ordinating and administering all of the individual budgets and will review and authorise each individual budget. The budget committee will normally be made up of senior executives and each function of the business should be represented on the budget committee in order to ensure that there is full communication between all areas of the business. The budget committee will normally be assisted by an accountant known as the budget accountant.

Budget holders

Budget holders are the managers within a business that are responsible for preparing each resource budget. In most cases the budget holder should be the manager who will also be responsible for ensuring that the activities meet the budget.

Master budget

The master budget is the final overall budget for all areas of the business. It is normally set out in the form of a budgeted income statement, budgeted statement of financial position and cash flow budget.

Task 3.4

Budgeting process

The budgeting process starts with the setting of the budget (forecast) for the key budget factor. This will frequently be the sales budget although, if manufacturing resources are the key budget factor, this may be the labour budget or machine hours budget. Once the key budget factor budget has been set then the production budget will be set by the production manager and the various other resource budgets set by the relevant budget holders.

Once the budget holder has drafted his budget then he will submit this to the budget committee. The budget officer will ensure that the budget is consistent with the other resource budgets, checking, for example, that it has been prepared in line with the production budget.

There will then frequently be negotiations between the budget committee and the budget holder regarding the detailed content of the budget. The manager might for example have built in an increase in costs over previous years which the budget committee does not agree with. The budget holder may well have to change his draft budget and re-submit it to the budget committee a number of times before the budget committee is satisfied with it.

Once the budget committee have agreed all of the resource budgets with the budget holders then they will be formed into the master budget.

Task 3.5

Rolling budget

A rolling budget is one which is constantly being updated and added to. It will be set in detail for the next short accounting period and in outline for the remainder of the 12-month period. As each accounting period passes, the details of the next period's budget are produced and the budget extended to maintain a 12-month coverage.

For example if budgets are set for each of 13 four-week periods in a year, initially the detailed budget will be set for period 1 and the remaining 12 periods' budgets will be in outline. Towards the end of period 1 the detail for period 2's budget will be set and the outline budget for period 1 of the following year added.

The benefits of a rolling budget are that the detailed budgeting only has to be performed for the next accounting period rather than for periods a long time in advance, therefore the budget is potentially more accurate. This makes it more useful to you when assessing the performance of the business by comparing actual results with the budgeted figures. It also means that when setting the detail of each period's budget, the budget holder can react to changes in circumstances that are revealed by comparison of the actual figures for each period to the budgeted figures.

Task 3.6

To: Managing Director
From: An Accountant
Subject: **The budgeting process**
Date: xx.xx.xx

The method of budgeting that is usually used may not be the most appropriate for the business.

Current method

The current method is incremental budgeting, as this takes the prior year budget and adjust the costs included for changes in price and level of output.

However, the activities of the business, and how these are carried out, may have changed significantly over recent years. For example, the production process may now use more advanced machinery, and less labour, leading to higher power, maintenance and depreciation costs, but lower labour costs. This means the costs may be out of date.

The current method of budgeting does not encourage costs savings or efficiencies, as inefficiencies and any budget slack are rolled forward year-on-year. As various costs are never kept within budget, with no apparent consequences, there is no motivation to stick to the budget.

Zero-based budgeting

An alternative would be to use zero-based budgeting. This looks at the costs of each cost centre from scratch for each period. Each cost is considered in the context of the production budget and the amount of each cost must then be specifically justified and not just included in the budget because it was in last year's budget.

For each item of activity which causes a cost, the following types of question must be asked:

- Is the activity necessary?
- Are there alternatives to this activity?
- What are the costs of the alternative?
- What would happen if the activity were not carried out?
- Is the expense of the activity worth the benefit?

By asking such questions, the activity and its related costs can either be justified for inclusion in the budget or a cheaper alternative found.

Using this method would therefore promote cost-savings and efficiencies, eliminate budgetary slack and motivate staff as the budget is realistic, but challenging.

Task 3.7

To: Managing Director
From: An Accountant
Date: xx.xx.xx
Subject: **The budgeting process**

Hi Jai,

I am e-mailing you with an explanation of how to improve the company's budgeting procedures:

(a) **(i)** At the moment the budgeting process is carried out by the accounts department. There would be a number of advantages if departments themselves were involved in the budget setting process. This is a bottom up approach and may allow for more accurate information as well as increasing motivation within each department.

(ii) Currently we use periodic budgeting where a budget is set for a period and is then reviewed after the period end. An alternative to this is rolling budgets, this is where budgets are updated on a regular basis (monthly or quarterly). This enables the company to be more flexible and to ensure adequate resources are available.

(b) In order to motivate managers to be more involved in preparing budgets the following methods might be considered: (**Note:** only two methods are required)

Departmental managers should be educated and trained so that they understand the importance of budgeting and how their departmental budget fits with the achievement of the overall objectives of H Ltd.

There should be recognition of the achievements of departments in meeting their budgets. This may be either financial or non-financial.

Similarly there should be an acknowledgement, that if targets are not met then, this too is noted by senior management.

The accounts department should offer support to departments when preparing their budgets.

Task 3.8

REPORT

To: Managing Director
From: Accountant
Date: xx.xx.xx
Subject: **Motivating managers**

Budgets are used to monitor and evaluate performance. Since managers are accountable for the actual performance compared with the budget, budgets can be used as a tool to motivate. However, this needs to be done carefully.

Managers should only be assessed on items that are within their control. A failure to do so may impact on the manager's motivation for achieving budgetary targets.

Bottom-up budgeting (in which managers have a degree of input into the budget) is also considered to help motivate managers. Managers are more motivated to achieve the budget because they have been involved in the planning process.

Budgets need to be attainable in order to be motivating. If a budget is seen as ideal and therefore impossible to achieve, this can have a demotivating effect. If a budget is set at a level which is challenging but attainable, then this can be motivating to the manager.

Performance related pay (such that managers' remuneration increases if they meet budgets and targets) is another way of motivating managers. However, the rewards being offered must be great enough to have an effect.

Chapter 4

Task 4.1

	✓
13,800	
13,200	✓
14,400	
2,100	
1,500	

Workings

	Units
Sales	13,800
Less opening inventory	(2,100)
Add closing inventory	1,500
Production	13,200

Task 4.2

	✓
189,500	✓
175,500	
210,500	
191,923	

Workings

	Units
Sales	200,000
Less opening inventory	(35,000)
Add closing inventory (70% × 35,000)	24,500
Production	189,500

Task 4.3

	✓
1,500 units	
1,875 units	
7,500 units	✓
9,000 units	

Workings

Opening inventory + production (P) – closing inventory = sales

1,500 + P – 0 = 1.2 × P

1,500 = 0.2 P

P = 7,500

Task 4.4

	✓
16,686	
16,702	✓
16,486	
15,714	

Workings

Production required = 16,200 × 100/97
= 16,702 units

Task 4.5

	Period 1	Period 2	Period 3
Opening inventory	2,700	2,875	2,750
Production	10,975	11,375	11,050
Subtotal	13,675	14,250	13,800
Sales	10,800	11,500	11,000
Closing inventory	2,875	2,750	2,800

Working

	Period 1 Units	Period 2 Units	Period 3 Units
Sales	10,800	11,500	11,000
Less opening inventory	(2,700)	(2,875)	(2,750)
Add closing inventory			
11,500 × 25%	2,875		
11,000 × 25%		2,750	
11,200 × 25%			2,800
Production units required	10,975	11,375	11,050

Task 4.6

	Period 1	Period 2	Period 3
Required units	12,000	11,000	12,500
Manufactured units	12,500	11,459	13,021

Working for example for period 1

12,000 × 100/96 = 12,500

If the answer is not a round number it must be rounded up to ensure sufficient units are produced.

Task 4.7

	✓
114,300 kg	
26,950 kg	
28,222 kg	
141,112 kg	✓

Workings

Materials usage:

	Kg
25,400 × 5 kgs	127,000
Add wastage 127,000 × 10/90	14,112
Raw material required	141,112

Task 4.8

The material usage budget for the raw material is [200,000] kgs.

The materials purchasing budget for the raw material is [194,000] kgs.

Workings

Materials usage budget:

40,000 units × 5 kgs = 200,000 kgs

Materials purchases budget:

	Kg
Raw materials required	200,000
Less opening inventory	(30,000)
Add closing inventory	
(30,000 × 80%)	24,000
	194,000

Task 4.9

	Period 1
Materials usage budget in kg	320,000
Materials purchases budget in kg	343,500
Materials purchases budget in £	858,750

Workings (Period 1)

Materials usage budget:

	Kg
Production 32,000 × 8 kgs	256,000
Normal loss 256,000 × 20/80	64,000
Materials usage	320,000

Materials purchasing budget – units:

	Kg
Materials usage	320,000
Less opening inventory	(64,000)
Add closing inventory	
35,000 × 8kg × 100/80 × 25%	87,500
	343,500

Materials purchasing budget – value

	£
343,500 kg × £2.50	858,750

Task 4.10

	✓
324 hours	
400 hours	✓
396 hours	
360 hours	

Working

One unit requires	18 × 100/90	=	20 hours
20 units require	20 × 20	=	400 hours

Task 4.11

	✓
400,000 hours	✓
384,000 hours	
100,000 hours	
480,000 hours	

Working

Standard hours	120,000 × 4	=	480,000 hours
Actual hours	480,000 × 100/120	=	400,000 hours

Task 4.12

For quarter 1, the production budget is [104,167] units.

For quarter 1, the labour usage budget is [603,073] hours.

Workings

Production budget

	Units
Sales	102,000
Less opening inventory	(17,000)
Add closing inventory (115,000 × 10/60)	19,167
Production	104,167

Labour usage budget

	Hours
Standard hours 104,167 × 5.5	572,919
Actual hours 572,919 × 100/95	603,073

Task 4.13

	Period 1
Sales budget (£)	120,000
Production budget (units)	3,176
Materials usage budget (kg)	14,116
Materials purchasing budget (kg)	15,530
Labour budget (hours)	7,940
Labour budget (£)	63,520

Workings

	Period 1 £
Sales budget (3,000 × £40)	120,000
Production budget	**Units**
Sales	3,000
Less opening inventory	(600)
Add closing inventory	
3,400 × 20%	680
	3,080
Defective units	
3,080 × 3/97 (rounded up)	96
	3,176
Materials usage budget	**Kg**
Production 3,176 × 4kg	12,704
Normal loss (× 10/90)	1,412
Materials usage	14,116
Materials purchasing budget	**Kg**
Materials usage	14,116
Less opening inventory	(4,200)
Add closing inventory	
16,040 × 35%	5,614
Purchases	15,530

	Period 1 £
Labour budget – hours	Hours
Standard hours	
Production 3,176 × 2	6,352
Idle time (hours x 20/80)	1,588
Total hours	7,940
Labour budget – £	
7,940 × £8	63,520

Task 4.14

- The number of production days are 60
- The closing finished inventory of Aye in units is 125
- The closing finished inventory of Bee in units is 200
- The labour hours available before overtime has to be paid are 29,400
- Production budget (units): Aye 1,495

  Bee 2,359
- Materials purchases budget (kg) 21,943
- Materials purchases budget (£) 219,430
- Labour usage budget (hours) 31,463
- Labour cost budget (£) 259,956
- The cost saving arising from the change in inventory levels for quarter 1 is

£	2,010

Workings

Production days = 12 × 5 = 60 days

Closing inventory of finished goods:

Aye = 1,500 × 5/60 = 125 units
Bee = 2,400 × 5/60 = 200 units

Labour hours available before overtime

= 12 weeks × 35 hours × 70 employees
= 29,400 hours

Production budget

	Aye Units	Bee Units
Sales	1,500	2,400
Less opening inventory	(160)	(300)
Add closing inventory	125	200
	1,465	2,300
Faulty production		
1,465 × 2/98	30	
2,300 × 2.5/97.5		59
	1,495	2,359

Materials purchases

	Kg
1,495 × 4 kg	5,980
2,359 × 7 kg	16,513
Material usage	22,493
Less opening inventory	(2,800)
Add closing inventory (22,493 × 6/60)	2,250
Materials purchases	21,943
Materials purchases budget – 21,943 × £10	£ 219,430
Labour budget – hours	

	Hours
Standard hours	
Aye 1,495 × 10 hours	14,950
Bee 2,359 × 7 hours	16,513
	31,463
Labour budget – value	
	£
Standard rate: (35 × 12 × 70) = 29,400 hours × £8	235,200
Overtime: (31,463 – 29,400) = 2,063 hours × £8 × 1.5	24,756
	259,956

Cost savings:

	Opening inventory	Closing inventory	Reduction	Saving £
Aye	160	125	35 × £6 =	210
Bee	300	200	100 × £7 =	700
Raw materials	2,800	2,250	550 × £2 =	1,100
				2,010

Task 4.15

		Period 1	Period 2	Period 3	Period 4
(i)	Gross production budget (units)	20,400	22,400	23,800	23,000
(ii)	Materials purchases budget (litres)	61,500	68,250	70,800	
(iii)	Materials purchases budget (£)	492,000	546,000	566,400	
(iv)	Labour budget (hours)	10,200	11,200	11,900	
(v)	Labour budget (£)	67,200	67,200	73,500	

(i) Gross production budget

	Period 1 Units		Period 2 Units		Period 3 Units		Period 4 Units	
Sales		19,400		21,340		23,280		22,310
Closing stock (W1)	4,268		4,656		4,462		4,462	
Opening stock	3,880		4,268		4,656		4,462	
Increase/ (decrease) in stock		388		388		(194)		–
Good production		19,788		21,728		23,086		22,310
Faulty production (W2)		612		672		714		690
Gross production		20,400		22,400		23,800		23,000

Workings

1 There are 20 days in each period.

Closing inventory = 4 days' sales in the next period = 4/20 of next period's sales

Closing inventory in period 1 = 4/20 × 21,340 =	4,268
Closing inventory in period 2 = 4/20 × 23,280 =	4,656
Closing inventory in period 3 = 4/20 × 22,310 =	4,462
Closing inventory in period 4 = 4/20 × 22,310 =	4,462

2 3% of gross production is scrapped. Good production therefore represents 97% (or 97/100) of gross production. Faulty production is 3% (or 3/100) of gross production and hence 3/97 of good production.

Faulty production is 3/97 × good production.

(ii) Materials purchases budget

	Period 1 Litres		Period 2 Litres		Period 3 Litres	
Material used in production (W1)		61,200		67,200		71,40C
Closing inventory (W2)	16,800		17,850		17,250	
Opening inventory	16,500		16,800		17,850	
Increase/(decrease) in inventory		300		1,050		(60C
Purchases (litres)		61,500		68,250		70,80C

Workings

1 Each unit requires three litres of material.

Material used in production = 3 × gross production (calculated in (i) above)

Material used in production, period 1 = 3 × 20,400 =	61,200
Material used in production, period 2 = 3 × 22,400 =	67,200
Material used in production, period 3 = 3 × 23,800 =	71,400

2
- There are 20 days in each period.
- Closing inventory must equal five days' gross production in the next period.
- Each unit requires three litres of material.
- Closing inventory in period 1 = 5/20 × 22,400 (from (i) above) × 3 = 16,800

  Closing inventory in period 2 = 5/20 × 23,800 × 3 = 17,850

  Closing inventory in period 3 = 5/20 × 23,000 × 3 = 17,250

(iii) Cost of material purchases

	Period 1	Period 2	Period 3
Material to be purchased (from (ii))	61,500 litres	68,250 litres	70,800 litres
Cost per litre	× £8	× £8	× £8
Cost of material purchases	£492,000	£546,000	£566,400

(iv) Labour budget

	Period 1	Period 2	Period 3
Gross production (units) (from (i))	20,400	22,400	23,800
Labour hrs required per unit	× 0.5	× 0.5	× 0.5
Labour hrs required	10,200	11,200	11,900

(v) Cost of labour budget

Labour hrs required	10,200	11,200	11,900
Basic labour hrs available *	11,200	11,200	11,200
Surplus hrs/ (overtime hrs)	1,000	–	(700)

* 70 workers × 40 hrs per wk × 4 wks = 11,200

	Period 1 £	Period 2 £	Period 3 £
Labour cost per period (guaranteed) *	67,200	67,200	67,200
Cost of overtime (700 × £9)	–	–	6,300
Cost of labour	67,200	67,200	73,500

* 70 workers × £240 × 4 wks

Task 4.16

(a)

Draft operating budget	Draft	Revision
Sales units (210,000 × 1.15)	210,000	241,500
	£	£
Sales price (7 × 0.9)	7.00	6.30
Sales revenue	1,470,000	1,521,450
Variable production costs (924,000 × 1.15)	924,000	1,062,600
Fixed production costs	325,000	325,000
Gross profit	221,000	133,850
Gross profit will decrease by		87,150

(b) Revised material cost (£427,500/0.95 × 0.9)

£	405,000

(c) Revised salary budget (£244,800/1.02 × 0.98)

£	235,200

Task 4.17

Budgeted units	Year	April
Units sold	216,000	18,200
Units produced	210,000	18,000

Budget in £	Year	April
Sales revenue	1,166,400	98,280
Material used	472,500	40,500
Direct labour	300,000	26,000
Variable production overhead	77,000	6,600
Fixed production overhead	13,200	1,100

Workings

Sales revenue £1,166,400/216,000 × 18,200 = £98,280

Materials used £472,500/210,000 × 18,000 = £40,500
Alternative: 18,000 × 3kg × £0.75 = £40,500

Labour

		Hrs
Hours required	(18,000 × 5mins)/60	1,250
Hours available		1,500
Overtime required		250

		£
Basic labour cost	1,250 × £16	20,000
Overtime	250 × £16 × 1.5	6,000
Total labour cost		26,000

Variable overhead

Annual hours required (210,000 × 5) / 60 = 17,500 hours
Variable overhead £77,000 / 17,500 hours × 1,500 hours = £6,600

Fixed overhead

£13,200 / 12 = £1,100

Task 4.18

	£	£
Revenue (25,000 × £6.50)		162,500
Less cost of sales:		
Direct materials 25,000 × 2kg × £0.75	37,500	
Direct labour 25,000 × 6/60 × £12	30,000	
Production overheads	16,000	
Cost of sales		(83,500)
Gross profit		79,000

Capital budget

	£
Capital purchase (car)	20,000
Total	20,000

Task 4.19

Budgetary slack

In the process of preparing budgets, managers might **deliberately overestimate costs and underestimate sales**, so that they will not be blamed in the future for overspending and poor results.

In controlling actual operations, managers must then **ensure that their spending rises to meet their budget**, otherwise they will be 'blamed' for careless budgeting.

Budget bias can **work in the other direction**, too. It has been noted that, after a run of mediocre results, some managers **deliberately overstate revenues and understate cost estimates**, no doubt feeling the need to make an immediate favourable impact by promising better performance in the future. They may merely delay problems, however, as the managers may well be censured when they fail to hit these optimistic targets.

Spending the full budget

Managers will often try to make sure that they **spend up to their full budget allowance, and do not overspend**, so that they will not be accused of having asked for too much spending allowance in the first place. A manager might be given an annual budget of £360,000. The manager knows that they will be punished for spending more than £360,000 but that if they spend less than £300,000 their budget will probably be reduced next year, leading to a loss of status and making their job more difficult next year.

Task 4.20

Product	Units	Hours per unit	Hours required
X	380	2.5	**950**
Y	440	1	**440**
Z	700	0.75	**525**
Total			**1,915**
Total machine hours available			**1,600**

4 machines, each operating for 400 hours = 1,600 machine hours. 1,915 hours are required, therefore **one** extra machine must be hired.

Chapter 5

Task 5.1

	October	November	December
Budgeted cash receipts from sales (£)	262,000	266,500	250,000

Workings

		October £	November £	December £
Cash sales	280,000 × 30%	84,000		
	250,000 × 30%		75,000	
	220,000 × 30%			66,000
Credit sales				
August	240,000 × 30%	72,000		
September	265,000 × 40%	106,000		
	265,000 × 30%		79,500	
October	280,000 × 40%		112,000	
	280,000 × 30%			84,000
November	250,000 × 40%			100,000
Total cash receipts		262,000	266,500	250,000

Task 5.2

	October	November	December
Budgeted cash payments for purchases (£)	174,490	182,450	199,620

Workings

		October £	November £	December £
August	180,000 × 35%	63,000		
September	165,000 × 45%	74,250		
	165,000 × 35%		57,750	
October	190,000 × 20% × 98%	37,240		
	190,000 × 45%		85,500	
	190,000 × 35%			66,500
November	200,000 × 20% × 98%		39,200	
	200,000 × 45%			90,000
December	220,000 × 20% × 98%			43,120
Total cash payments		174,490	182,450	199,620

Task 5.3

	August	September	October
Budgeted cash payments to suppliers (£)	150,000	156,000	165,000

Workings

	August £	September £	October £
July purchases 5,000 × £50 × 60%	150,000		
August purchases 5,200 × £50 × 60%		156,000	
September purchases 5,500 × £50 × 60%			165,000

Task 5.4

Assume no opening and closing inventory.

Forecast annual sales of £6,000 and a mark up of 33⅓%, means forecast purchases of

£	4,500

Forecast annual purchases of £12,000 and a margin of 20%, means forecast sales of

£	15,000

Forecast annual sales of £16,000 and forecast annual profits of £6,000, mean forecast mark-up of [60] % and margin of [37.5] %.

Workings

Tutorial note. In this question you are told that there is no opening and closing inventory, therefore purchases = cost of sales. 1/3

Remember **mark up** is on **purchases**.

If purchases 100%, mark up 33⅓,

Sales = 100 + 33⅓ = 133⅓%

$$\text{Purchases} = \frac{100}{133\frac{1}{3}} \times 6{,}000$$

$$= £4{,}500$$

Remember **margin** is on **sales**.

If sales 100% margin 20%

Purchases = 100 – 20 = 80%

$$\text{Sales} = \frac{100}{80} \times 12{,}000$$

$$= £15{,}000$$

$$\text{Mark up} = \frac{\text{Profits}}{\text{Purchases}}$$

$$= \frac{6{,}000}{16{,}000 - 6{,}000}$$

$$= 60\%$$

$$\text{Margin} = \frac{\text{Profits}}{\text{Sales}}$$

$$= \frac{6{,}000}{16{,}000}$$

$$= 37\tfrac{1}{2}\%$$

Task 5.5

	April	May	June
Budgeted cash receipts for sales (£)	600,500	560,650	539,375

Workings

		April £	May £	June £
March sales	650,000 × 70%	455,000		
April sales	600,000 × 25% × 97%	145,500		
	600,000 × 70%		420,000	
May sales	580,000 × 25% × 97%		140,650	
	580,000 × 70%			406,000
June sales	550,000 × 25% × 97%			133,375
Total cash receipts		600,500	560,650	539,375

Task 5.6

	April	May	June
Budgeted cash wages payments (£)	19,740	18,060	16,800

Workings

Production budget

	March Units	April Units	May Units	June Units
Sales next month	7,200	7,050	6,550	6,150
Less opening inventory	(1,000)	(1,000)	(1,000)	(900)
Add closing inventory	1,000	1,000	900	750
Production in units	7,200	7,050	6,450	6,000

Labour budget hours

	April Hours	May Hours	June Hours
7,050/3	2,350		
6,450/3		2,150	
6,000/3			2,000

Labour budget – £

	April £	May £	June £
Hours × £8.40	19,740	18,060	16,800

Task 5.7

Cash budget – July to September

	July £	August £	September £
Opening balance	(82,000)	(42,420)	(23,254)
Cash receipts:			
Sales (W1)	438,400	467,840	488,520
Proceeds from sale of equipment	0	7,500	0
Total receipts	438,400	475,340	488,520
Cash payments:			
Purchases (W2)	246,000	256,000	288,000
Wages	60,000	60,000	60,000
Overheads (W3)	44,000	47,750	49,000
Selling expenses	48,000	50,000	52,000
Equipment	0	42,000	0
Overdraft interest	820	424	233
Total payments	398,820	456,174	449,233
Closing balance	(42,420)	(23,254)	16,033

Workings

1 **Receipts from credit sales**

		July £	August £	September £
April sales	420,000 × 12%	50,400		
May sales	400,000 × 25%	100,000		
	400,000 × 12%		48,000	
June sales	480,000 × 40%	192,000		
	480,000 × 25%		120,000	
	480,000 × 12%			57,600
July sales	500,000 × 20% × 96%	96,000		
	500,000 × 40%		200,000	
	500,000 × 25%			125,000
August sales	520,000 × 20% × 96%		99,840	
	520,000 × 40%			208,000
September sales	510,000 × 20% × 96%			97,920
		438,400	467,840	488,520

2 **Payments to suppliers**

		July £	August £	September £
May purchases	250,000 × 60%	150,000		
June purchases	240,000 × 40%	96,000		
	240,000 × 60%		144,000	
July purchases	280,000 × 40%		112,000	
	280,000 × 60%			168,000
August purchases	300,000 × 40%			120,000
		246,000	256,000	288,000

3 **Overheads**

		July £	August £	September £
June overheads	(50,000 – 6,000) × 25%	11,000		
July overheads	(50,000 – 6,000) × 75%	33,000		
	(50,000 – 6,000) × 25%		11,000	
August overheads				
	(55,000 – 6,000) × 75%		36,750	
	(55,000 – 6,000) × 25%			12,250
September overheads				
	(55,000 – 6,000) × 75%			36,750
		44,000	47,750	49,000

Task 5.8

Tutorial note. Don't get caught out by putting all the rent in the budget.

Cash budget: July to September

	July £000	August £000	September £000
Opening balance	(112)	(60)	184
Cash receipts:			
Sales	160	320	80
Cash payments:			
Purchases	60	40	120
Salaries	36	36	36
Rent (£48,000 ÷ 4)	12	–	–
Total payments	108	76	156
Closing balance	(60)	184	108

Task 5.9

Cash budget – October to December

	October £	November £	December £
Opening balance	40,000	45,020	43,020
Cash receipts:			
Sales (W1)	378,000	391,500	417,000
Cash payments:			
Purchases of raw materials (W2)	144,180	156,060	164,880
Wages (W3)	118,800	127,440	131,760
Production overheads	50,000	50,000	50,000
General overheads	60,000	60,000	68,000
Total payments	372,980	393,500	414,640
Closing balance	45,020	43,020	45,380

Workings

1 **Receipts from credit sales**

	October £	November £	December £
August sales			
5,000 × £75 × 60%	225,000		
September sales			
5,100 × £75 × 40%	153,000		
5,100 × £75 × 60%		229,500	
October sales			
5,400 × £75 × 40%		162,000	
5,400 × £75 × 60%			243,000
November sales			
5,800 × £75 × 40%			174,000
	378,000	391,500	417,000

2 Purchases of raw materials

Production budget

	Aug Units	Sept Units	Oct Units	Nov Units	Dec Units
Sales	5,000	5,100	5,400	5,800	6,000
Less opening inventory	(500)	(500)	(500)	(600)	(700)
Add closing inventory	500	500	600	700	800
Production	5,000	5,100	5,500	5,900	6,100

Purchases budget

	Aug Kg	Sept Kg	Oct Kg	Nov Kg
Required for next month's production × 3 kg	15,300	16,500	17,700	18,300
Less opening inventory	(3,000)	(3,000)	(3,000)	(3,200)
Add closing inventory	3,000	3,000	3,200	3,500
Purchases in kg	15,300	16,500	17,900	18,600
	£	£	£	£
Kg × £9	137,700	148,500	161,100	167,400

Payments to suppliers

	October £	November £	December £
August purchases			
137,700 × 40%	55,080		
September purchases			
148,500 × 60%	89,100		
148,500 × 40%		59,400	
October purchases			
161,100 × 60%		96,660	

	October £	November £	December £
161,100 × 40%			64,440
November purchases			
167,400 × 60%			100,440
Total payments to suppliers	144,180	156,060	164,880

3 **Wages**

Labour budget – hours

	Oct	Nov	Dec
Production units (W2)	5,500	5,900	6,100
× 3 hours = labour usage (hours)	16,500	17,700	18,300
	£	£	£
Wages – production × £7.20	118,800	127,440	131,760

Task 5.10

Cash flows in respect of sales

£	232,400

Cash flows in respect of purchases

£	120,800

Workings

Cash inflows from sales = opening receivables + sales – closing receivables

= £23,000 + £228,400 – £19,000 = £232,400

Cash outflows on purchases = opening payables + purchases – closing payables

= £5,600 + £128,000 – £12,800 = £120,800

Chapter 6

Task 6.1

	✓
Sales demand	
Material	
Machine hours	✓
Labour hours	

The business can sell 12,000 units.

The business has enough material to make 25,000/2 = 12,500 units.

The business has enough machine hours (5 × 1,000 = 5,000 hours) to make 5,000/0.5 = 10,000 units.

The business has enough labour hours (40 × 500 = 20,000 hours) to make 20,000/1.5 = 13,333 units.

Therefore, the machine hours limit production to 10,000 units despite the sales demand being greater than this.

Task 6.2

The number of units that can be produced in total is [25,800].

The number of units that can be produced each month is [2,150].

Workings

Total production = $\frac{129{,}000 \text{ kgs}}{5 \text{ kgs}}$

= 25,800 units

Monthly production = $\frac{25{,}800}{12}$

= 2,150 units

Task 6.3

Purchasing plan 1:

	July	Aug	Sept	Oct	Nov	Dec
Requirement	4,800	4,300	4,100	4,900	4,200	5,000
Purchase	4,500	4,300	4,100	4,500	4,200	4,500
Shortage	300	–	–	400	–	500

Total shortage = 300 + 400 + 500

= 1,200 kgs

Purchasing plan 2:

	July	Aug	Sept	Oct	Nov	Dec
Requirement	4,800	4,300	4,100	4,900	4,200	5,000
Purchase	4,500	4,500	4,500	4,500	4,500	4,500
Excess/(Shortage)	(300)	200	400	(400)	300	(500)
Inventory	–	200	600	200	500	–
Production	4,500	4,300	4,100	4,900	4,200	5,000

Total shortage: 300 kgs

By purchasing the maximum available in August, September and November, even though it is not required, the shortages in October and December can be covered from materials held in inventory. This leaves only the 300 kg shortage in July.

Task 6.4

(a) If the shortage is only temporary then there are a number of short-term solutions which could alleviate the problem.

- Using inventory of materials – the inventory of raw materials could be run down in order to maintain production and sales.
- Using inventory of finished goods – in order to maintain sales in the short-term, finished goods inventory can be run down even though production levels are not as high as would be liked.

- Rescheduling purchases – if the amount of the raw material required is available in some periods but not in others, then the raw materials purchases could be rescheduled to ensure that the maximum use is made of the available materials.

(b) If the shortage is a long-term problem then the following are possible options for the business.

- Seeking an alternative supplier – this is an obvious solution but it may not always be possible to find another supplier who can supply the correct quality at an acceptable price.
- Finding an alternative material – in some instances a product can only be made from one particular material but it may be possible to adapt the design of the product and the manufacturing process in order to use a substitute material that is widely available.
- Manufacturing an alternative product – it may be possible to switch the production process to manufacture an alternative product which uses a different material which is not in short supply.
- Buying in finished goods for resale – instead of producing the product, it could be purchased in finished form from another producer who is not having the same problems with supply of the materials required. However this probably would lead to an under-utilisation of production resources and a major change in the organisation's strategy.

Task 6.5

Purchasing plan:

	May	June	July	Aug	Sept	Oct
Material requirement	9,500	10,200	10,200	9,300	10,200	10,300
Potential shortage	–	200	200	–	200	300

Do not buy 10,000 kgs each month as this will lead to inventory that is not required. However buy enough in May and August to cover the potential shortages.

	May	June	July	Aug	Sep	Oct
Material requirement	9,500	10,200	10,200	9,300	10,200	10,300
Potential shortage	0	200	200	0	200	300
Purchases	9,900	10,000	10,000	9,800	10,000	10,000
Inventory	400	(200)	(200)	500	(200)	(300)
Production	9,500	10,200	10,200	9,300	10,200	10,300

Total shortage: 0 kgs

Task 6.6

The maximum level of production each week is 184 units.

Working

Total hours available (including overtime)	=	12 × (38 + 8)
	=	552 hours per week
Maximum production	=	552/3
	=	184 units

Possible solutions to this problem could be:

- Increase the overtime worked – it may be possible to agree additional overtime with the employees in order to maintain production; however at 46 hours per week already, this may not be an option here.
- Recruit more skilled employees – Skilled labour is currently short. If this is to be a long-term problem it may be more cost effective to recruit more skilled labour resource than to use temporary staff or sub-contractors.
- Use sub-contractors – in some types of business it may be possible to use agency workers or to sub-contract the work in order to maintain production levels. This option is likely to be fairly costly and should only be used if this is a short-term problem.
- Use up finished goods inventory – if production levels are lower than required to meet sales demand, then for the short term sales can still be maintained by running down the finished goods inventory. This is not, however, a long-term solution.

- Buying in finished goods inventory – this could be an expensive option leaving factory capacity under-utilised and may have quality implications as well.
- Improving labour efficiency – this is not something that can be done quickly but with training over a period of time it may be possible to increase the number of employees with the skills required.

Task 6.7

	✓
1,840	✓
3,740	
7,440	
5,600	

Working

Labour hours required	=	1,860 units × 4 hours
	=	7,440 hours
Labour hours available	=	160 employees × 35 hours
	=	5,600 hours
Overtime hours required	=	7,440 – 5,600
	=	1,840 hours

Task 6.8

The maximum production for a week is 4,200 units.

Working

Hours of production line time	=	2 shifts × 7 hours × 5 days × 2 production lines
	=	140 hours
Maximum production	=	140 hours × 30 units
	=	4,200 units

If sales demand exceeds this maximum production level there are a number of options that could be considered.

- Introduce a third shift so that the production lines are in fact running for 21 hours a day.
- Lengthen the shift to, say, a 9 hour shift.

- Operate the factory for 6 or even 7 days a week.
- Speed up the production line so that more units are produced an hour.

Task 6.9

Any three of the following:

- Limitations on the amount of raw materials that can be purchased.
- Manpower limitations – a limit to the number of hours that can be worked in the period by the labour force.
- Capacity limitations – a limit to the number of machine hours available.
- A limit to the quantity that can be produced by a production line in the period.

Task 6.10

	Key budget factor
A private nursing home with 140 beds. The home is situated in an area which has a large proportion of retired people amongst the population and there is little difficulty in recruiting suitable staff.	Number of beds available
A vendor of ice cream in a busy shopping centre. The transportable stall can store a maximum of 50 litres of ice cream.	Quantity of ice cream that can be stored per day
A partnership of three skilled craftsmen making carved chess sets from wood and marble for home sales and exports to specific order. Sales demand is high and orders have to be frequently rejected.	Number of partner hours available
A manufacturer of home cinema sound systems which are similar to those of other manufacturers and who distributes the systems amongst a number of small high street electrical retailers.	Demand from retail stores

Reasoning

There would appear to be no limits regarding demand for beds or the labour force. The key budget factor would seem to be the number of beds available.

In a busy shopping centre demand for the ice cream is probably not the key factor therefore it is likely to be the quantity of ice cream that can be stored each day.

Sales demand is not a limiting factor however as this is highly skilled work the available hours of the three partners will be the key budget factor.

As the products are similar to those of other manufacturers and therefore can be replaced by similar products by the retail stores then it is highly likely that the demand from the retail stores will be the key budget factor.

Task 6.11

	Production units
Product W	300
Product X	250
Product Y	0
Product Z	1,000

Workings

	W (£)	X (£)	Y (£)	Z (£)
Sales price	200	90	180	150
Materials cost	(60)	(24)	(57)	(36)
Labour (hours)	(24)	(30)	(72)	(36)
Contribution	116	36	51	78

Kg/unit	20	8	19	12
Contribution/kg	£5.80	£4.50	£2.68	£6.50
Rank	2	3	4	1
Production	300	250	0	1,000
Kg used in production	6,000	2,000	0	12,000

Chapter 7

Task 7.1

	✓
£60,000	
£20,000	✓
£15,000	
£19,800	

£15,000 is the cost of 3 supervisors therefore each one costs £5,000 per period.

At a production level of 330,000 units four production supervisors will be required costing £20,000 for the period.

Task 7.2

Material cost (112,000 × £2.40) (W)

£	268,800

Labour cost (112,000 × £1) + £24,000 (W)

£	136,000

Production overhead (fixed)

£	38,000

Working

Materials	100,000 units	£2.40 per unit
	120,000 units	£2.40 per unit

Therefore a variable cost – £2.40 per unit

Labour	100,000 units	£1.24 per unit
	120,000 units	£1.20 per unit

Therefore a semi-variable cost

Variable element	=	£20,000/20,000 units
	=	£1 per unit

At 100,000 units:	£
Variable cost	100,000
Fixed cost (bal fig)	24,000
Total cost	124,000

Task 7.3

If the actual activity level is 72,000 units, the flexed budget figure for production overhead is

£	608,000

Working

Production overhead (72,000 × £7) + £104,000 = £608,000

Variable element of cost $= \dfrac{£664{,}000 - 524{,}000}{20{,}000 \text{ units}} =$ £7 per unit

At 60,000 units:	£
Variable element 60,000 × £7	420,000
Fixed element (bal fig)	104,000
Total cost	524,000

Task 7.4

	Budget 20,000 units £	Flexed budget 15,000 units £
Sales	130,000	97,500
Material (W1)	(55,000)	(41,250)
Labour (W2)	(35,000)	(28,000)
Production overhead	(18,000)	(18,000)
Gross profit	22,000	10,250
General expenses (W3)	12,000	10,450
Operating profit/(loss)	10,000	(200)

Workings

1 Material

£55,000 /20,000 units = £2.75 per unit
£2.75 × 15,000 units = £41,250

2 Labour

15,000 units /2,000 units = 8 operatives required
8 × £3,500 = £28,000

3 General expenses

Variable cost per unit: (£12,000 – £6,400) /20,000 = £0.27
∴ £6,400 + (£0.27 × 15,000) = £10,450

Task 7.5

	Flexed budget 230,000 units		Actual 230,000 units		Variances
	£	£	£	£	£
Sales		1,564,000		1,532,000	32,000 (A)
Materials	793,500		783,200		10,300 (F)
Labour	433,500		428,600		4,900 (F)
Production expenses	180,000		173,500		6,500 (F)
Production cost		1,407,000		1,385,300	
Gross profit		157,000		146,700	10,300 (A)
General expenses		72,000		74,700	2,700 (A)
Operating profit		85,000		72,000	13,000 (A)

Working

Sales – variable $= \dfrac{£1{,}360{,}000}{200{,}000} = \dfrac{£1{,}632{,}000}{240{,}000}$

$= £6.80$ per unit

Materials – variable cost $= \dfrac{£690{,}000}{200{,}000} = \dfrac{£828{,}000}{240{,}000}$

$= £3.45$ per unit

Labour – semi-variable cost

Variable element $= \dfrac{£449{,}000 - 387{,}000}{40{,}000}$

$= £1.55$

Fixed element $= £387{,}000 - (200{,}000 \times 1.55)$

$= £77{,}000$

At 230,000 $= £77{,}000 + (230{,}000 \times 1.55)$

$= £433{,}500$

Production expenses – semi-variable cost

Variable element $= \dfrac{£186{,}000 - 162{,}000}{40{,}000}$

$= £0.60$ per unit

Fixed element	=	£162,000 – (200,000 × 0.60)
	=	£42,000
At 230,000	=	£42,000 + (230,000 × 0.60)
	=	£180,000

Task 7.6

Quarter 2 budget

	£	£
Sales 50,000 units		400,000
Materials	165,400	
Labour	69,800	
Cost of production: 56,000 units @ £4.20	235,200	
Less: closing inventory	25,200	
Cost of sales		210,000
Contribution		190,000
Production overhead		56,000
General expenses		52,000
Operating profit		82,000

	£
Profit per absorption costing budget	88,000
Less production overhead included in closing inventory (6,000 × £1)	(6,000)
Profit per marginal costing budget	82,000

Task 7.7

The standard material price is £ [3.40] per kg.

Workings

Direct material price variance

	£
6,850 kg used should have cost (× standard cost)	A
But did cost	21,920
Direct material price variance	1,370 Favourable

Now we need to think about what number A must be to give a favourable variance of £1,370. If the variance is favourable then the actual cost ('did cost') was lower than it should be. This means we need to add £1,370 to £21,920 to get 'should cost'. So the materials should have cost £1,370 + £21,920 = £23,290.

We also know that

6,850 kg used should have cost (× standard cost) = £23,290

Now we can work out what the standard rate was: £23,290/6,850 = £3.40 per kg

Task 7.8

The actual quantity of material used is [51] kg.

The standard labour rate is £ [13] per hour.

Workings

The first thing to do with questions like these is to lay out variances in the way you would normally calculate them and then fill in the numbers that the question has given you.

We are given the materials price variance and the actual cost of material so we can start as if we were calculating the materials price variance:

Direct material price variance

	£
Actual kg used should have cost (× £15)	A
But did cost	615
Direct material price variance	150 (F)

Now we need to think about what number A must be to give a favourable variance of £150. If the variance is favourable then the actual cost ('did cost') was lower than it should be. This means we need to add £150 to £615 to get 'should cost'. So the materials should have cost £150 + £615 = £765.

We also know that:

Actual kg used should have cost (× £15) = £765

Now we can work out how many kg we actually used: £765/£15 = 51 kg

We can do the same for the labour rate variance.

Labour rate variance	£
575 hrs should have cost (× standard rate)	B
But did cost	7,835
Rate variance	360 (A)

Now we need to think about what number B must be to give an adverse variance of £360. If the variance is adverse then the actual cost ('did cost') was higher than it should be. This means we need to deduct £360 from £7,835 to get 'should cost'. So the materials should have cost £7,835 – £360 = £7,475.

We also know that

575 hrs should have cost (× standard rate) = £7,475

Now we can work out what the standard rate was: £7,475/575 = £13 per hour.

Task 7.9

The marketing or sales overhead variance may be favourable if the sales director is not immediately replaced, as the cost of the salary of the director is not incurred. However, if costs of recruitment are incurred, there may be an adverse administration or HR overhead variance.

There will be no effect on the sales variance, even if the volume sold decreases as the variance will be calculated after the budget has been flexed to actual activity levels.

Task 7.10

An adverse administrative overheads variance may be reported. This is because the administrative overheads will have increased as the salary of the credit controller would still have been paid while the external agency was also paid. The adverse variance may also be increased by the increase in irrecoverable debts if there was a break between the credit controller taking sick leave and the external agency being appointed.

Task 7.11

The importance of identifying controllable variances is in the area of motivation or de-motivation of management. If variances are reported, as part of the responsibility of a manager, over which he has no control, then this will have a de-motivational effect. If a manager is constantly held responsible for an adverse variance in a cost, the level of which he cannot influence, then this will not have a positive effect on the performance of this manager.

Investigating the causes of variances and determining any interdependence between the variances is an important aspect of management control because in a system of responsibility accounting the managers responsible for various elements of the business will be held accountable for the relevant variances. However they should only be held accountable for variances that are within their control.

There may be variances caused by factors which are beyond the manager's control, such as an increase in rent or business rates. There may also be variances in a manager's responsibility centre which have not been caused by his actions but by those of another responsibility centre manager.

An example is a favourable material price variance caused by purchasing a lower grade of material which leads directly to an adverse materials usage variance, as the lower grade of material means that there is greater wastage. The initial reaction might be to give credit to the purchasing manager for the favourable variance and to lay blame for the adverse usage variance on the production manager. However the true picture is that, in the absence of any further reasons for the variance then the responsibility for both variances lies with the purchasing manager.

Task 7.12

Units	Flexed budget 34,000		Actual 34,000		Variance A/F
	£	£	£	£	£
Sales (34,000 × £22) (W)		748,000		697,000	51,000 (A)
Direct costs					
Materials (34,000 × £8.40) (W)	285,600		299,200		13,600 (A)
Factory power (34,000 × £2.10) (W)	71,400		68,000		3,400 (F)
Subtotal		357,000		367,200	
Contribution		391,000		329,800	
Labour	180,000		192,600		12,600 (A)
Factory power	20,600		20,600		–
Fixed overheads	75,000		79,000		4,000 (A)
Fixed costs		275,600		292,200	
Operating profit		115,400		37,600	77,800 (A)

Workings

Budgeted unit selling price $= \dfrac{£660{,}000}{30{,}000}$

= £22 per unit

Budgeted unit material cost $= \dfrac{£252{,}000}{30{,}000}$

= £8.40 per unit

Marginal element of factory power = £83,600 – £20,600

= £63,000

Budgeted marginal cost per unit $= \dfrac{£63{,}000}{30{,}000}$

= £2.10 per unit

Actual marginal cost = £88,600 – £20,600

= £68,000

Explanation of why the flexed budget operating statement shows different results from that of the original budget

The original budget was a fixed budget based upon the budgeted sales and production of 30,000 units. The flexed budget is based upon sales and production of 34,000 units therefore the anticipated increases in sales revenue and variable costs is built into this budget.

Task 7.13

Flexed budget statement

	Flexed budget	Actual results	Variances A/F	Variances A/F
Production and sales volume (car stereos)	140,000	140,000		
	£000	£000	£000	%
Conversion costs				
Labour (W1)	1,000	972	28 (F)	3%
Light, heat and power (W2)	610	586	24 (F)	4%
Rent, rates and insurance (W3)	200	200	–	–
Depreciation (W4)	150	132	18 (F)	12%
Total conversion costs	1,960	1,890	70 (F)	4%
Bought-in materials (W5)	2,800	3,220	420 (A)	–15%
Total expenses	4,760	5,110	350 (A)	–7%
Sales revenue (W6)	5,600	6,440	840 (F)	15%
Operating profit	840	1,330	490 (F)	58%

Workings

Budgeted selling price per car stereo = revenue/sales volume

(£3,200,000/80,000 or £4,000,000/100,000) £40.00

Budgeted bought-in material cost per car stereo = bought-in materials/ production volume (£1,600,000/80,000 or £2,000,000/100,000) £20.00

Labour unit variable cost

Using the incremental approach:

	Volume		Cost
	100,000		£760,000
	80,000		£640,000
Incremental volume of	20,000	has an incremental cost of	£120,000

Therefore variable labour cost per unit = £120,000/20,000 = £6 per unit

Budgeted total labour fixed cost

	£
Total cost	760,000
Total variable cost (£6 × 100,000)	600,000
Fixed cost	160,000

An identical answer is possible by using the total cost for 80,000 car stereos and deducting the total variable cost based on 80,000 car stereos.

Budgeted variable cost of light, heat and power

Using the incremental approach:

	Volume		Cost
	100,000		£450,000
	80,000		£370,000
Incremental volume of	20,000	has an incremental cost of	£80,000

Therefore variable cost per unit = £80,000/20,000 = £4 per unit

Budgeted total light, heat and power fixed cost

	£
Total cost	450,000
Total variable cost (£4 × 100,000)	400,000
Fixed cost	50,000

An identical answer is possible by using the total cost for 80,000 car stereos and deducting the total variable cost based on 80,000 car stereos.

Workings for flexed budget

1 Variable cost of 140,000 car stereos + labour fixed cost = (£6 × 140,000) + £160,000 = £1,000,000

2 Variable cost of 140,000 car stereos + light, heat and power fixed cost = (£4 × 140,000) + £50,000 = £610,000

3 Fixed cost so the same at all levels of production

4 Fixed cost so the same at all levels of production

5 Cost of 140,000 car stereos = £20 × 140,000 = £2,800,000

6 Sales revenue from 140,000 car stereos = £40 × 140,000 = £5,600,000

MEMO

To: Chief Executive
From: Assistant management accountant
Date: xx.xx.xx
Subject: **Performance related pay**

Possible reasons for improved profit

The improved profitability may have occurred even without the introduction of performance related pay.

(1) The company cannot control the volume of sales as the only customer is the parent company. It therefore depends entirely on the level of demand from the parent company. This year they required 40,000 more car stereos than budgeted and so, even without performance related pay, the sales volume target would have been exceeded. All other things being equal (ie no increase in fixed costs and variable costs per unit), this increase in demand would have increased profit.

(2) Part of the improved profit arose from an apparent change in accounting policy on depreciation. There were no non-current asset purchases or sales and hence the actual annual depreciation figure would have been known and should have been the same as the budgeted figure. The actual figure was less than the budgeted figure and so actual profit was greater than budgeted.

(3) The selling price per car stereo is set at twice the cost of the bought-in materials. This means the more managers pay for the bought-in materials, the higher the price they can charge the parent company and so the higher the profit we can report. (Such a policy leads to inefficiencies, however, as managers are motivated to pay as much as possible for bought-in materials.)

(4) Fixed costs are the same irrespective of the level of production and sales. Hence the contribution will increase, all other things being equal, if actual

volumes are greater than budgeted volumes and, with fixed costs remaining constant, so will profitability.

Note. You were required to provide only three reasons.

General conditions for improved performance

There are several conditions necessary if performance related pay is to lead to improved performance.

(1) Managers need to know the objectives of the organisation.

(2) Budgets must tie in with those objectives.

(3) Managers must feel that the objectives are achievable (although they should provide a challenge).

(4) Managers must want to achieve those objectives.

(5) Managers must be able to influence the achievement of the objectives.

(6) The level of rewards – both financial and non-financial – should motivate managers.

(7) Managers must have the skills necessary to achieve the targets.

(8) There should be a short period of time between effort and reward.

(9) The actual results should not be capable of being manipulated.

Note. You were required to provide only three reasons.

Task 7.14

REPORT

To: Managing Director
From: Accountant
Date: xx.xx.xx
Subject: **November production cost variances**

One explanation for the variances may have been the labour grade that was used in production for the month. It was a more junior grade than normal because of staff shortages. This has given an overall favourable labour variance, meaning the reduction in rate made up for any labour inefficiencies (extra hours) caused by using a lower grade. However, it may also have contributed to the high adverse materials variances if such staff caused more materials wastage.

For future months, we should either ensure that we have enough of the normal grade of labour or we should train the junior grade staff.

The high adverse materials variance will have been caused by an increase in the price of our materials. As it is believed that this is a permanent price increase by all suppliers, we should consider altering the materials standard cost to reflect this; otherwise each month, we will have adverse materials variances.

The factory now has an additional rent cost which has presumably caused the adverse fixed overhead variance. If the additional inventory requirement and hence, the additional rent, is a permanent change then this should be built into the budgeted fixed overhead figure.

Task 7.15

REPORT

To: Managing Director
From: Accountant
Date: xx.xx.xx
Subject: **Reasons for variances**

(a) Possible reasons for the variances

- Direct materials (carrots) price variance

  The price variance for the carrots is £1,750 adverse. Soupzz Ltd is unable to control the price that it pays for its carrots as this is in part due to the weather. As there was bad flooding Soupzz had to find a supplier further away which appears to have pushed up the price resulting in an adverse variance.

- Direct materials (carrots) usage variance

  The usage variance for the carrots is £760 favourable. Due to the flooding, the regular suppliers were unable to provide the carrots demanded and as a result Soupzz Ltd had to look for alternative suppliers. They found suppliers who were able to provide a sweeter type of carrot, which resulted in less usage to obtain a similar soup taste and a favourable variance.

  As a result of the change to sweeter carrots, fewer carrots were used in the production process. It would be useful to understand whether this had an impact on the taste of the soup to the consumer.

- Direct materials (potatoes) price variance

  The price variance for the potatoes is £450 favourable. There was a change in the general level of demand for potatoes which led to a reduction in price by the supplier. This had a positive impact for Soupzz and lowered the price they paid for the potatoes required.

- Direct materials (potatoes) usage variance

  The potatoes usage variance is £1,700 adverse. There was no change in the quality of the potatoes but the increase in usage of potatoes is due to the change in the sweetness of the carrots.

(b) During the machine downtime some of the labour staff had nothing to do. They have therefore been paid for more hours than they actually worked. This results in an idle time variance. As there was no idle time expected, this is an adverse idle time variance. The variance is the number of hours of idle time multiplied by the standard rate per hour.

Chapter 8

Task 8.1

Number of:

- Website hits per day
- Purchases per day
- Purchases per hit
- Customer accounts
- Returns per order

Task 8.2

• A vet's surgery	–	animals seen per day
• A bar	–	drinks served per employee
• A firm of solicitors	–	chargeable hours as a percentage of total hours
• A retail store	–	sales per employee
	–	sales per square metre of shop floor
• A wedding cake business	–	number of cakes made per day
	–	number of cakes decorated per day

Task 8.3

- Weight of shavings collected per day.
- Cost of shavings collected per day.
- Weight of shavings collected per machine.
- Cost of storage of shavings before collection for scrap.
- Frequency/cost of rubbish collection service.

Task 8.4

- Chargeable time of a trainee as a percentage of time spent in the office
- Cost of non-chargeable hours (because of training or lack of chargeable time in office)
- Cost of training per trainee
- Average time from joining firm to exam completion

Task 8.5

- Units produced per machine hour
- Total maintenance costs, and maintenance costs per machine
- Breakdowns (and so idle hours) per machine, or total lost machine hours per week/month
- Number of machines in operation per shift

Task 8.6

- Complaints per number of covers
- Time between order and meals being served

Task 8.7

Driver productivity

A possible measure of driver productivity is the number of miles per driver, or the number of journeys undertaken per driver.

Satisfaction of passenger needs indicators, using the information collected

The satisfaction of passenger needs could be monitored by the number of passengers per journey.

Depending on the size of the buses, passenger needs may be less satisfied if there are more passengers per journey because of more crowding or the need to stand because no seats were available.

Another measure of the satisfaction of passenger needs is the number of journeys per day, as this may mean reduced waiting times.

Satisfaction of passenger needs indicators, which would require other information

A measure of the satisfaction of customer needs that cannot be derived from the existing data is cleanliness of the buses.

Monitoring the cleaning cost per day or per bus might give some indication of the effort put into keeping the buses clean.

Another measure of the satisfaction of customer needs **is punctuality** of the buses and their **adherence to published** timetables.

Monitoring the percentage of buses arriving and departing within five minutes of their published time would give an indication of performance in this area.

Safety indicators, using existing information

The safety aspect of Travel Bus's operations could be monitored by the maintenance cost per mile, although a high cost may in fact indicate an older fleet, and so reduced safety.

Safety indicators, requiring other information

A measure of the safety aspect that cannot be derived from the existing data is the number of accidents per year.

Another measure could be the percentage of maintenance cost that is incurred to prevent faults compared with the percentage incurred to correct faults. This would indicate whether faults were being prevented before they occurred, or whether maintenance was being carried out 'after the event', which could compromise safety.

Task 8.8

		20X7	20X8
% of customers complaining	(12 / 480)	2.5%	
	(26 / 650)		4.0%
Returning customers (4 visits)	(425 / 480)	88.5%	
	(420 / 650)		64.6%

Task 8.9

The number of complaints has gone up from 2.5% to 4% per customer and the number of returning customers has fallen from 88.5 % to just 64.6%.

This may be due to the inexperience of the new member of the team.

It could also be due to the fact that Billy has hired a lower skilled worker (as he is paying him £15,000 per year and the other workers £20,000 per year on average).

The existing team members have not received a pay rise, so they may not be as motivated as in the prior year and hence not delivering the same level of service as that offered previously.

Task 8.10

Machine utilisation rates

Machine time per unit

Idle hours

Machine maintenance cost per unit

Production cost per unit

AAT AQ2016 SAMPLE ASSESSMENT 1 MANAGEMENT ACCOUNTING: BUDGETING

Time allowed: 2 hours and 30 minutes

The AAT may call the assessments on their website, under study support resources, either a 'practice assessment' or 'sample assessment'.

Management Accounting: Budgeting (MABU) AAT sample assessment 1

Task 1 (20 marks)

You are gathering budget information for the company for which you work.

(a) Match each item of budget data below with its appropriate source.

(CBT instructions: To show each answer, click on a box in the left column then click on a box in the right column. To remove a line, click on it.)

(3 marks)

Budget data	**Appropriate source**
Current pay rates of your company's staff	Customer Relationship Management (CRM) system
Competitors' prices	Government statistics (eg ONS in the UK)
Retail price index for the country in which we operate	Internet search
	A website for a leading business news and information organisation (eg The Financial Times' website)
	Payroll records

As a budget accountant, you require information in order to complete the tasks below.

(b) Match each task with the individual or group that you will need to contact for information. *(CBT instructions: To show each answer, click on a box in the left column then click on a box in the right column. To remove a line, click on it.)*

(4 marks)

Task	Task
Agree planning assumptions for budget preparation	Purchasing manager
Explain a labour efficiency variance	Production manager and human resources manager
Draft the direct labour cost budget	Budget committee
Propose budget pay rates	Production manager
	Human resources manager

(c) Select the appropriate accounting treatment for each of the following items.

(6 marks)

Preparing plans for factory extension

[▼]

Repairs to sales office furniture

[▼]

Raw material usage

[▼]

Production labour – overtime pay

[▼]

Product advertising

[▼]

Replacement of production machinery

Drop-down list:

Activity based charge to products
Allocate to administration overheads
Allocate to marketing overheads
Capitalise and depreciate over useful life
Charge to production in a labour hour overhead rate
Charge to production in a machine hour overhead rate
Direct cost

(d) Select the appropriate term to match the following description.
(1 mark)

Collecting data about a proportion of the items in the population to indicate the characteristics of the whole population.

Drop-down list:

Census
Market analysis
Market research
Product life cycle
Sampling
Stratified sampling
Trend

(e) The budget committee has set the sales volume growth and pricing assumptions for years 2, 3, 4 and 5 in the form of indices.

Complete the sales revenue forecast below. Do not show decimals. Round each figure to the nearest whole number.

(6 marks)

	Year 1	Year 2	Year 3	Year 4	Year 5
Sales volume index	140.0	148.0	152.6	156.0	160.0
Sales price index	112.0	115.0	120.0	125.0	130.0

Sales revenue	Actual year 1 £	Forecast year 2 £	Forecast year 3 £	Forecast year 4 £	Forecast year 5 £
At Year 1 prices	384,000				
At expected prices					

Task 2 (20 marks)

(a) Complete the following production forecast for product G.

Round any decimal figures up to the next whole number of units, if necessary.

(10 marks)

- Closing inventory should be 30% of the following week's sales volume.
- 8% of all production fails quality control checks and is rejected.

Production (units)	Week 1	Week 2	Week 3	Week 4	Week 5
Opening inventory	20,000				
Good production					
Sales volume	68,000	69,000	67,000	70,000	72,000
Closing inventory					
Rejected production					
Total manufactured units					

You have the following information:

- 61,000 items of product W will be manufactured next week.
- Each item requires 11 kilograms of raw material.
- 5% of raw material is wasted during manufacture.
- The opening inventory will be 84,000 kilograms.
- The closing inventory will be 80,000 kilograms.

(b) Calculate material purchases.

Round up to the next whole number of kilograms, if necessary.

(i) How many kilograms are required for input to production? **(1 mark)**

[ ] kg

(ii) How many kilograms must be purchased? **(1 mark)**

[ ] kg

You have the following information:

- 88,000 items of product ZZ will be manufactured in July.
- 25 items are made in one labour hour.
- 15 staff will each work 180 basic hours.

(c) How many overtime hours should be budgeted?

Round up to the next whole number of hours, if necessary. **(1 mark)**

[ ] hours

You have the following information:

- There are 90 machines in the department
- Each can be used for 240 hours in the period
- 9,750 items are to be made
- Each item requires 2 hours of machine time

(d) What is the machine utilisation?

Do not show decimals. Round to the nearest percentage, if necessary. **(2 marks)**

[ ] %

According to the standard cost card, each unit of this product requires:

- 8 kilograms of material
- 45 minutes of direct labour time
- 12 minutes of machine time

Budgets have been drafted by departmental heads which show:

- Maximum sales demand of 720 units
- 6,000 kilograms of material available
- 450 hours of direct labour time available without using overtime
- 140 hours of machine time available

(e) **Calculate the capacity constraints for product JJ by completing the table below.**

Round down to the maximum whole number of units, if necessary. **(5 marks)**

Production capacity	Units
Sufficient materials are budgeted to manufacture:	
Without overtime, sufficient direct labour is budgeted to manufacture:	
Sufficient machine time is budgeted to manufacture:	
Without overtime, the maximum sales volume is:	
With unlimited overtime, the maximum sales volume is:	

Task 3 (20 marks)

(a) **Complete the three working schedules using the information from the production budget and notes below. Enter all figures as positive values.** **(9 marks)**

Production budget	Units
Opening inventory of finished goods	26,200
Production	348,000
Sub-total	374,200
Sales	340,000
Closing inventory of finished goods	34,200

Materials

- Each unit produced requires 0.7 kilograms (kg) of material.
- Closing inventory will be valued at the budgeted purchase price per kg.

Labour

- Each item takes 5 minutes to produce.
- 164 staff work 160 basic hours each in the period.
- Overtime is paid at 40% above the basic hourly rate.

Production overhead

- Variable overhead is recovered on total labour hours

Materials	Kg	£
Opening inventory	8,800	12,320
Purchases @ £1.45 per kg		
Sub-total		
Used in production		
Closing inventory	7,400	

Labour	Hours	£
Basic time @ £15.00 per hour		
Overtime		
Total		

Production overhead	Hours	£
Variable @ £2.60 per hour		
Fixed		94,660
Total		

(b) Complete the operating budget.

Enter income, costs and inventories as positive figures.

(6 marks)

Closing finished goods inventory will be valued at the budgeted production cost per unit.

Operating budget	Units	£ per unit	£
Sales revenue		3.95	
Cost of goods sold			**£**
Opening inventory of finished goods			70,740
Cost of production		**£**	
Materials			
Labour			
Production overhead			
Closing inventory of finished goods			
Cost of goods sold			
Gross profit/(loss)			
Overheads		**£**	
Administration		112,000	
Marketing		168,000	
Operating profit/(loss)			

(c) Complete the cash flow forecast using the budget data that you have calculated in parts (a) and (b) of this task and the additional information below.

Enter receipts and payments as positive figures. (5 marks)

- The sale receivables balance is expected to decrease by £12,000 over the year.
- The materials payable balance is expected to increase by £4,000 over the year.
- All other payments are made in the year in which they are incurred.
- Production overheads include a depreciation charge of £25,000.

Cash flow forecast		£
Opening cash balance/(overdraft)		(8,000)
Sales receipts		
Payments:	£	
Material		
Labour		
Production overheads		
Other overheads		
Capital expenditure	75,000	
Closing cash balance/(overdraft)		

Task 4 (20 marks)

You are the budget accountant of a manufacturing business.

You have prepared a draft budget for the cost of fuel oil for the coming year. The sales and production volume budgets have already been agreed.

Fuel oil is used to power the production process and to provide heating in the administrative and sales areas. The consumption for production and for heating are metered separately.

New machines, which will be more fuel efficient, are being installed for production and additional insulation has been put in place to cut heating costs. The chief engineer has calculated the expected savings in fuel oil consumption from both of these improvements.

Fuel oil prices have fluctuated between 48p per litre and 79p per litre during the last two years. The chief buyer thinks that fuel oil prices are set to rise and that it would be prudent to budget at 72p.

Draft fuel oil cost budget	This year actual	Next year budget
Production budget	**Units**	**Units**
Production volume	63,000	64,575
Fuel oil consumption	**Litres**	**Litres**
Per 1,000 units of production	750	600
Total for production	47,250	38,745
Total for heating	7,800	7,020
Total consumption	55,050	45,765
Fuel oil cost	**£**	**£**
Per litre (average)	0.60	0.72
Total for year	**33,030**	**32,951**

Write an email to the budget committee, in three sections:

(a) Submit the draft budget for approval and explain the key planning assumptions. (10 marks)

(b) Explain why planning assumptions in this draft budget are not totally within the control of management. (5 marks)

(c) Recommend four performance measures that could be reported on a regular basis to help management keep fuel oil costs within budget. (5 marks)

To:	The Budget Committee	**Date:**	xx.xx.xx
From:	Budget Accountant	**Subject:**	**Draft fuel oil cost budget**

(a) Budget submission

(b) Control

(c) Performance measures

Budget Accountant

Task 5 (20 marks)

(a) Select the appropriate term to match each of these descriptions. **(2 marks)**

Description	Term
Detailed budgets prepared by functional managers are collated to form a master budget	▼
A cost that fluctuates in direct proportion to changes in activity	▼

Drop-down list:

Bottom-up budgeting
Budget flexing
Budget revision
Fixed cost
Incremental budgeting
Rolling budgets
Semi-variable cost
Stepped cost
Top-down budgeting
Variable cost
Zero base budgeting

(b) Calculate the sales revenue and production cost budget for April using the information provided. (7 marks)

- Each unit is made from 0.85 kilograms (kg) of material costing £2.60 per kg.
- Each unit requires 10 minutes of direct labour time.
- 3,300 hours of basic time is available in April. Any extra hours must be worked as overtime.
- The direct labour rate is £15 per hour and the overtime premium is 40%.
- Variable production overhead relates to labour hours, including overtime.
- Fixed production overheads are incurred at a steady monthly rate across the year.

Budgeted units	Year	April
Unit sold	238,000	20,000
Unit produced	246,000	21,000

Budget in £	Year	April
Sales revenue	1,594,600	
Costs of production:		
Material used	543,660	
Direct labour	623,400	
Variable production overhead	95,940	
Fixed production overhead	96,000	
Total production cost	1,359,000	

You have submitted a draft operating budget to the budget committee. The committee has asked you to budget for an alternative scenario and calculate the increase or decrease in expected profit.

(c) Complete the alternative scenario column in the operating budget table and calculate the increase or decrease in profit.

For the sales price per unit figure, enter any decimal places, if relevant.

For the other figures, round to the nearest whole number, if necessary. **(11 marks)**

Assumptions in the first scenario:

- Material and labour costs are variable.
- Depreciation is a stepped cost, increasing at every 6,000 units.
- There is an allowance for an energy price rise of 7.5%.

Alternative scenario:

- Increase the selling price by 5%.
- Reduce the sales volume by 8%.
- Revise the energy price rise to 10%.

Operating Budget	First draft	Alternative scenario
Sales price per unit (£)	12.00	
Sales volume	80,000	
	£	£
Sales revenue	960,000	
Costs:		
Material	392,000	
Labour	224,000	
Energy	43,000	
Depreciation	42,000	
Total	701,000	
Gross profit	259,000	
Increase/(decrease) in gross profit		

Task 6 (20 marks)

(a) Select the appropriate term to match the following description. **(2 marks)**

A financial measure of the difference between budget and actual performance.

Drop-down list:

Labour efficiency variance
Labour rate variance
Material usage variance
Performance indicator
Variance
Variance analysis

The operating statement for October showed that direct raw material costs were £142,560. 9,900 kg of material were used and 6,000 items were made and sold. The standard cost allows 1.6 kilograms (kg) of material for each item at a standard price of £14.50 per kg.

(b) Complete the table of direct raw material costs, indicating whether each variance is favourable or adverse. (10 marks)

Direct raw material costs		Favourable/Adverse
Flexed budget (standard cost)	£	
Actual material price per kg (correct to £0.01)	£	
Actual material used per item (correct to two decimal places)	kg	
Price variance	£	▼
Usage variance	£	▼
Cost variance	£	▼
Cost variance percentage (correct to one decimal place)	%	

Drop-down list:

Adverse
Favourable

(c) Prepare the direct labour cost statement from the activity data provided. (8 marks)

Round to the nearest whole number if necessary.

Activity data	Items produced	Labour hours	Cost £
Budget	18,300	3,660	65,880
Actual results	18,800	4,700	82,720

Direct labour cost statement	£
Standard labour cost of production	
Variances	**£ Fav / (Adv)**
Labour rate	
Labour efficiency	
Labour cost	

Task 7 (20 marks)

In this task you are required to complete a monthly operating report. The original budget and actual results have been entered.

You have the following information:

- Material, labour, quality control and distribution costs are variable.
- Energy cost is semi-variable. The fixed element is budgeted at £18,000 for the month.
- Equipment hire is a stepped cost, budgeted to increase at every 25,000 units of monthly production.
- Other production overheads include a variable element of £0.40 per unit.
- All other costs are fixed.

Complete the Monthly Operating Report below by flexing the budget, calculating all variances and showing whether each variance is favourable or adverse.

Show adverse variances as negative figures using minus signs or brackets.

Variance totals are calculated for you automatically. (20 marks)

Monthly Operating Report

Original budget		Flexed budget	Actual	Variance Fav / (Adv)
73,000 (units)	Sales and production volume		76,000 (units)	
£		£	£	£
1,306,700	Sales revenue		1,285,600	
	Costs:			
357,700	Materials		373,800	
306,600	Labour		317,900	
21,900	Quality control		23,600	
18,250	Distribution		18,800	
29,680	Energy		33,200	
37,500	Equipment hire		43,850	
11,900	Depreciation		12,400	
46,400	Other production overheads		46,300	
73,000	Marketing		75,600	
63,000	Administration		64,200	
965,930	Total		1,009,650	0
340,770	Operating profit/(loss)		275,950	0

Task 8 (20 marks)

Review the operating statement shown below, and the additional information below, and then prepare a report by email.

Operating statement	Flexed budget	Actual	Variance (Fav/(Adv)
Sales volume		635,000 pairs	
	£000	£000	£000
Sales revenue	**1,080**	**1,111**	**31**
Variable costs			
Material	305	356	(51)
Labour	368	413	(45)
Distribution	38	41	(3)
Power	25	24	1
Production overhead	76	83	(7)
Total	**812**	**917**	**(105)**
Contribution	**268**	**194**	**(74)**
Fixed costs			
Depreciation	11	12	(1)
Other production overhead	21	19	2
Marketing	22	21	1
Administration	29	31	(2)
Total	**83**	**83**	**0**
Operating profit	**185**	**111**	**(74)**

The business makes and sells a range of leather gloves. The gloves are made by hand in two different styles, each from three alternative grades of leather. All six products are produced in small, medium and large sizes.

The gloves are sold to department stores. The selling price are negotiated by the sales manager.

The original budget was based on production and sales of 630,000 pairs of gloves and showed an operating profit of £183,000. In the operating statement, the budget has been flexed in proportion to the actual number of pairs of gloves made and sold.

There has been a noticeable shift in demand throughout the year, with increasing sales of gloves in the more intricate of the two styles. There has also been increasing demand for gloves made with the best grade of leather.

The sales of small and medium size gloves have been greater than expected whilst sales of the large size have declined.

Management accounts are prepared promptly at each month end, comparing results with a monthly flexed budget. There is no costing system.

The chief executive is alarmed by the poor profit performance and asks you, the Budget Accountant, to review the effectiveness of the budgetary control system.

Write an email to the Chief Executive, covering the following three areas:

(a) Explain the reasons for the variances of sales revenue, materials and labour. (10 marks)

(b) Described the information that the sales manager requires from the accounting system to help him create a rational pricing policy. (5 marks)

(c) Describe any failings that you perceive in the budgetary control process and suggest how budgetary control could be improved. (5 marks)

To:	The Chief Executive	**Date:**	xx.xx.xx
From:	Budget Accountant	**Subject:**	**Performance review**

(a) Reasons for variances

(b) Information for pricing

(c) Budgetary control process

Budget Accountant

AAT AQ2016 SAMPLE ASSESSMENT 1 MANAGEMENT ACCOUNTING: BUDGETING

ANSWERS

Management Accounting: Budgeting (MABU) AAT sample assessment 1

Task 1 (20 marks)

(a) Match each item of budget data below with its appropriate source.

(CBT instructions: To show each answer, click on a box in the left column then click on a box in the right column. To move a line, click on it.)

(3 marks)

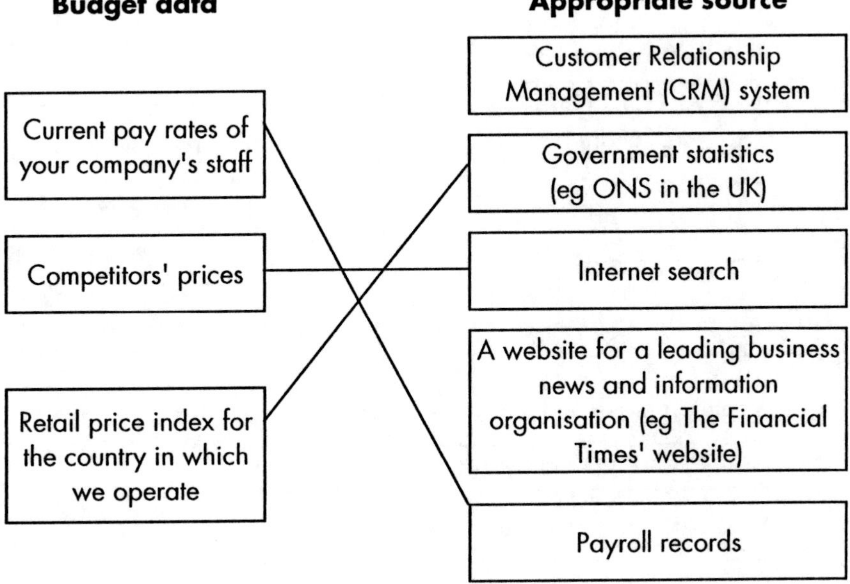

(b) Match each task with the individual or group that you will need to contact for information. *(CBT instructions: To show each answer, click on a box in the left column then click on a box in the right column. To remove a line, click on it.)* **(4 marks)**

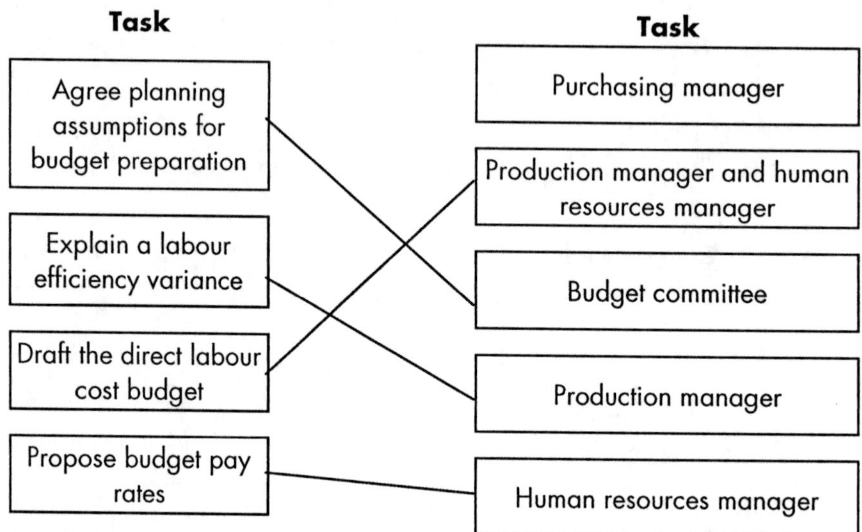

(c) Select the appropriate accounting treatment for each of the following items. **(6 marks)**

Preparing plans for factory extension

Capitalised and depreciate over useful life

Repairs to sales office furniture

Allocate to marketing overheads

Raw material usage

Direct cost

Production labour – overtime pay

Direct cost

Product advertising

Allocate to marketing overheads

Replacement of production machinery

Capitalised and depreciate over useful life

(d) Select the appropriate term to match the following description. (1 mark)

Collecting data about a proportion of the items in the population to indicate the characteristics of the whole population.

Sampling

The budget committee has set the sales volume growth and pricing assumptions for years 2, 3, 4 and 5 in the form of indices.

(e) Complete the sales revenue forecast below.

Do not show decimals. Round each figure to the nearest whole number. (6 marks)

	Year 1	Year 2	Year 3	Year 4	Year 5
Sales volume index	140.0	148.0	152.6	156.0	160.0
Sales price index	112.0	115.0	120.0	125.0	130.0

Sales revenue	Actual year 1 £	Forecast year 2 £	Forecast year 3 £	Forecast year 4 £	Forecast year 5 £
At Year 1 prices	384,000	405,943	418,560	427,886	438,857
At expected prices		416,816	448,457	477,551	509,388

Task 2 (20 marks)

(a) Complete the following production forecast for product G.

Round any decimal figures up to the next whole number of units, if necessary. (10 marks)

- Closing inventory should be 30% of the following week's sales volume.
- 8% of all production fails quality control checks and is rejected.

Production (units)	Week 1	Week 2	Week 3	Week 4	Week 5
Opening inventory	20,000	20,700	20,100	21,000	
Good production	68,700	68,400	67,900	70,600	
Sales volume	68,000	69,000	67,000	70,000	72,000
Closing inventory	20,700	20,100	21,000	21,600	
Rejected production	5,974	5,948	5,905	6,140	
Total manufactured units	74,674	74,348	73,805	76,740	

(b) Calculate material purchases.

Round up to the next whole number of kilograms, if necessary.

(i) How many kilograms are required for input to production? (1 mark)

706,316 kg

(ii) How many kilograms must be purchased? (1 mark)

702,316 kg

(c) Calculate overtime hours.

Round up to the next whole number of hours, if necessary. (1 mark)

How many overtime hours should be budgeted?

820 hours

(d) Calculate machine utilisation.

Do not show decimals. Round up to the next whole number of hours or percentage, if necessary. (2 marks)

What is the machine utilisation?

90 %

(9,750 × 2)/(90 × 240) × 100 = 90%

(e) Calculate the capacity constraints for product JJ by completing the table below.

Round down to the maximum whole number of units, if necessary. (5 marks)

Production capacity	Units
Sufficient materials are budgeted to manufacture:	750
Without overtime, sufficient direct labour is budgeted to manufacture:	600
Sufficient machine time is budgeted to manufacture:	700
Without overtime, the maximum sales volume is:	600
With unlimited overtime, the maximum sales volume is:	700

Task 3 (20 marks)

(a) Complete the three working schedules using the information from the production budget and notes below. Enter all figures as positive values. (9 marks)

Materials	Kg	£
Opening inventory	8,800	12,320
Purchases @ £1.45 per kg	242,200	351,190
Sub-total	251,000	363,510
Used in production	243,600	352,780
Closing inventory	7,400	10,730

Labour	Hours	£
Basic time @ £15.00 per hour	26,240	393,600
Overtime	2,760	57,960
Total	29,000	451,560

Production overhead	Hours	£
Variable @ £2.60 per hour	29,000	75,400
Fixed		94,660
Total		170,060

(b) Complete the operating budget.

Enter income, costs and inventories as positive figures. (6 marks)

Operating budget	Units	£ per unit	£
Sales revenue	340,000	3.95	1,343,000
Cost of goods sold			£
Opening inventory of finished goods			70,740
Cost of production		£	
Materials		352,780	
Labour		451,560	
Production overhead		170,060	974,400
Closing inventory of finished goods			95,760
Cost of goods sold			949,380
Gross profit/(loss)			393,620
Overheads		£	
Administration		112,000	
Marketing		168,000	280,000
Operating profit/(loss)			113,620

(c) Complete the cash flow forecast using the budget data that you have calculated in parts (a) and (b) of this task and the additional information below.

Enter receipts and payments as positive figures. (5 marks)

Cash flow forecast		£
Opening cash balance/(overdraft)		(8,000)
Sales receipts		1,355,000
Payments:	£	
Material	347,190	
Labour	451,560	
Production overheads	145,060	
Other overheads	280,000	
Capital expenditure	75,000	1,298,810
Closing cash balance/(overdraft)		48,190

Task 4 (20 marks)

Write an email to the budget committee, in three sections:

(a) Submit the draft budget for approval and explain the key planning assumptions. (10 marks)

(b) Explain why planning assumptions in this draft budget are not totally within the control of management. (5 marks)

(c) Recommend four performance measures that could be reported on a regular basis to help management keep fuel oil costs within budget. (5 marks)

(a) Budget submission

I attach the draft fuel oil cost budget for your consideration and approval. This is calculated from the agreed sales and production volume budget, which shows a 2.5% increase over this year. Fuel oil is used to power the production process and for heating.

The chief engineer has estimated the savings arising from the installation of fuel efficient production equipment (20% of the usage per 1,000 items) and improved insulation (10% of the heating requirement). We have assumed that the production element is a variable cost (varying in direct proportion to production volume) and that the heating element is a fixed cost (not varying with production volume, although it will fluctuate depending on weather conditions).

You will be aware of the recent volatility of energy prices. The chief buyer has recommended that we budget at 72p per litre which is 20% more than the average price this year.

Despite higher sales, we are budgeting for a very slight saving in fuel oil cost next year.

(b) Control

Management cannot control all of the variables in this budget.

- The sales and production budgets have already been approved but, of course, sales will be influenced by competitor activity and demand in the market.
- The price per litre of the fuel oil will depend on world energy prices and could vary considerably from the chief buyer's estimate, unless he is prepared to enter into a fixed tariff agreement.
- The usage of fuel oil for heating will be influenced by the weather.
- There is the inevitable possibility of error when estimating efficiency savings, but it is reasonable to hold management accountable for achieving the anticipated usage reductions for production and heating.

(c) Performance measures

There are four variable factors in this budget and they need to be monitored closely. I recommend that we regularly report and review the following measures:

- The purchase price of fuel oil in pence per litre
- Weekly production and sales volumes, in units
- The consumption of fuel oil for production, in litres per 1,000 units of production
- The consumption of fuel oil for heating, in litres per week or month

Whereas the first three of these can be compared against budget assumptions, the heating usage will be seasonal and should be compared against this year's usage to ensure that the expected savings are achieved.

Budget Accountant

Task 5 (20 marks)

(a) Select the appropriate term to match each of these descriptions. (2 marks)

Description	Term
Detailed budgets prepared by functional managers are collated to form a master budget	Bottom-up budgeting
A cost that fluctuates in direct proportion to changes in activity	Variable cost

(b) Calculate the sales revenue budget and production cost budget for April using the information provided. (7 marks)

Budgeted units	Year	April
Unit sold	238,000	20,000
Unit produced	246,000	21,000

Budget in £	Year	April
Sales revenue	1,594,600	134,000
Cost of production:		
Material used	543,660	46,410
Direct labour	623,400	53,700
Variable production overhead	95,940	8,190
Fixed production overhead	96,000	8,000
Total production cost	1,359,000	116,300

(c) **Complete the alternative scenario column in the operating budget table and calculate the increase or decrease in profit.**

For the sales price per unit figure, enter any decimal places, if relevant.

For the other figures, round to the nearest whole number, if necessary. **(11 marks)**

Operating Budget	First draft	Alternative scenario
Sales price per unit (£)	12.00	12.6
Sales volume	80,000	73,600
	£	£
Sales revenue	960,000	927,360
Costs:		
Material	392,000	360,640
Labour	224,000	206,080
Energy	43,000	44,000
Depreciation	42,000	39,000
Total	701,000	649,720
Gross profit	259,000	277,640
Increase/(decrease) in gross profit		18,640

Task 6 (20 marks)

(a) Select the appropriate term to match the following description. (2 marks)

A financial measure of the difference between budget and actual performance.

Variance

(b) Complete the table of direct raw material costs, indicating whether each variance is favourable or adverse. (10 marks)

Direct raw material costs		Favourable/Adverse
Flexed budget (standard cost)	£139,200	
Actual material price per kg (correct to £0.01)	£14.4	
Actual material used per item (correct to two decimal places)	1.65 kg	
Price variance	£990	Favourable
Usage variance	£4,350	Adverse
Cost variance	£3,360	Adverse
Cost variance percentage (correct to one decimal place)	2.4%	

(c) Prepare the direct labour cost statement from the activity data provided. (8 marks)

Round to the nearest whole number if necessary.

Activity data	Items produced	Labour hours	Cost £
Budget	18,300	3,660	65,880
Actual results	18,800	4,700	82,720

Direct labour cost statement	£
Standard labour cost of production	67,680
Variances	**£ Fav/(Adv)**
Labour rate	1,880
Labour efficiency	–16,920
Labour cost	–15,040

Task 7 (20 marks)

Complete the Monthly Operating Report below by flexing the budget, calculating all variances and showing whether each variance is favourable or adverse.

Show adverse variances as negative figures using minus signs or brackets. **(20 marks)**

Monthly Operating Report

Original budget		Flexed budget	Actual	Variance Fav/(Adv)
73,000	Sales volume (units)		76,000	
£		£	£	£
1,306,700	Sales revenue	1,360,400	1,285,600	–74,800
	Costs:			
357,700	Materials	372,400	373,800	–1,400
306,600	Labour	319,200	317,900	1,300
21,900	Quality control	22,800	23,600	–800
18,250	Distribution	19,000	18,800	200
29,680	Energy	30,160	33,200	–3,040
37,500	Equipment hire	50,000	43,850	6,150
11,900	Depreciation	11,900	12,400	-500
46,400	Other production overheads	47,600	46,300	1,300
73,000	Marketing	73,000	75,600	–2,600
63,000	Administration	63,000	64,200	–1,200
965,930	Total	1,009,060	1,009,650	–590
340,770	Operating profit/(loss)	351,340	275,950	–75,390

Task 8 (20 marks)

Write an email to the Chief Executive, covering the following three areas:

(a) Explain the reasons for the variances of sales revenue, materials and labour. (10 marks)

(b) Described the information that the sales manager requires from the accounting system to help him create a rational pricing policy. (5 marks)

(c) Describe any failings that you perceive in the budgetary control process and suggest how budgetary control could be improved. (5 marks)

(a) Reasons for variances

The operating statement shows a profit of £111,000 which is 39% below the original budget, despite better than anticipated sales volume and average selling price. Profit is 40% below the flexed budget. There are three significant variances.

Sales revenue shows a favourable variance of £31,000 (2.9%) which must be due to price, as the budget has been flexed. The average selling price has increased to £1.75 per pair as a result of a shift in demand towards our premium products.

Material costs were £51,000 (17%) above the flexed budget. This can be attributed to increased demand for gloves made from best quality leather. There may also be other price or efficiency factors but our accounting system does not provide an analysis. Similarly, we cannot tell what cost reduction has resulted from the shift towards smaller glove size, using less leather.

Labour costs were £45,000 (12%) above budget. Again, the shift in demand is the most likely cause as we are selling more gloves of the intricate design which, presumably, requires more handwork. This might have involved overtime working. Again, there could be other general wage rate or efficiency factors but we do not have the data to analyse.

(b) Information for pricing

The sales manager needs to know what it costs to make each of the products in the range. The average variable cost in the budget was £1.28 per pair but the actual cost was £1.44. If, as seems likely, this increase is due to a change in the product mix, the variation in cost between the products must be considerable. The fact that profit has dipped indicates that pricing has not been optimal. If premium products are underpriced demand will switch to them and production costs will rise disproportionately.

Costs are likely to vary according to the quality of leather used, the glove style and glove size. As fixed costs are a small proportion of the total we can focus on variable cost and contribution.

The shift in demand towards premium products should be good news for the business and enhance profitability. The contribution on each pair of the premium gloves should be at least as good, preferably better, than average.

The accounting system needs to identify the variable cost of each product in the range so that the sales manager can set prices that are both competitive and profitable across the range.

(c) Budgetary control process

Flexible budgeting is a powerful control tool in a single product environment but is of limited value if there is a diverse product range. Indeed it can produce misleading information.

Budgetary control could be improved by using standard costing. This would provide detailed cost data and analysis at product level. Standard costing can be fully integrated with budgeting to provide excellent control in a multi-product environment.

Standard costs should be calculated for each of the 18 products in the range (2 styles × 3 leather grades × 3 sizes). A costing system must be put in place to collect the actual costs of each product.

This will improve control by facilitating the reporting of variances. For instance, material cost variances could be analysed into price variances for each leather grade and usage variances for each glove style and size. Similar analyses could be made for other variable costs.

Standard costing will also provide the data to build realistic budgets and to inform sales pricing as described above in section 2 of this email.

Budget Accountant

AAT AQ2016 SAMPLE ASSESSMENT 2 MANAGEMENT ACCOUNTING: BUDGETING

AAT AQ2016 SAMPLE ASSESSMENT 2

You are advised to attempt sample assessment 2 online from the AAT website. This will ensure you are prepared for how the assessment will be presented on the AAT's system when you attempt the real assessment. Please access the assessment using the address below:

www.aat.org.uk/training/study-support/search

The AAT may call the assessments on their website, under study support resources, either a 'practice assessment' or 'sample assessment'.

BPP PRACTICE ASSESSMENT 1 MANAGEMENT ACCOUNTING: BUDGETING

Time allowed: 2.5 hours

PRACTICE ASSESSMENT 1

Management Accounting: Budgeting BPP practice assessment 1

Task 1 (20 marks)

(a) Match each item of budget data with its appropriate source.

(CBT instructions: Click on a box in the left column, then on one in the right column. To remove a line, click on it.) **(3 marks)**

Budget data
Corporation tax rates
Competitors' financial performance
Inflation rates

Appropriate source
Trade Union
HM Revenue & Customs
Financial Times
Internet search
Statistics published by Government (eg Office for National Statistics in UK)

As budget accountant, you require information in order to complete the tasks below.

(b) Match each task with the individual or group that you will need to contact for information. **(4 marks)**

(CBT instructions: Click on a box in the left column, then on one in the right column. To remove a line, click on it.)

Task
Obtain details of salaries for proposed new staff
Agree variance reports required for budget
Draft the direct materials budget
Obtain details of promotional activity

Contact
Budget committee
Marketing manager
Human resources manager
Trade union representative
Production manager

(c) Select the appropriate accounting treatment for each of the following items. (6 marks)

Cost	Accounting treatment
Repairs to head office furniture	▼
Water used directly in production	▼
Head office extension	▼
Raw material purchases	▼
Production labour – overtime pay	▼
Replacement of head office IT system	▼

Picklist:

Activity based charge to products
Allocate to administration overheads
Capitalise and depreciate over useful life
Charge to production in a machine hour overhead rate
Direct cost

(d) Select the appropriate term to match the following description. (1 mark)

Description	Term
Cost or income data collected over a number of periods, which may be used as a basis for forecasting	▼

Picklist:

Moving average
Product life cycle
Seasonal variation
Time series

The budget committee has set the sales volume growth and pricing assumptions for years 2, 3, 4 and 5 in the form of indices.

(e) Complete the sales revenue forecast below. Do not show decimals. Round each figure to the nearest whole number.

(6 marks)

	Year 1	Year 2	Year 3	Year 4	Year 5
Sales volume index	110.0	117.5	123.6	131.4	140.0
Sales price index	105.0	110.0	115.0	120.0	125.0
	Actual year 1	**Forecast year 2**	**Forecast year 3**	**Forecast year 4**	**Forecast year 5**
At year 1	856,000				
At expected prices					

Task 2 (20 marks)

(a) Complete the following production forecast for product J based on the information below. Do not show decimals. Round any decimal figures *up to the next whole number* of units.

(10 marks)

Closing inventory should be 12.5% of the following week's sales volume.

17.5% of all production fails quality control checks and is rejected.

Production (units)	Week 1	Week 2	Week 3	Week 4	Week 5
Sales volume	500	550	600	650	700
Opening inventory	100				
Closing inventory					
Saleable production					
Rejected production					
Total manufactured units					

(b) Calculate raw material requirements.

Do not show decimals. Round any decimal figures *up to the next whole number* of litres.

900 units of product N are to be manufactured next week.

Each requires 15 litres of raw material.

9% of raw material is wasted during manufacture.

The opening inventory will be 500 litres.

The closing inventory will be 600 litres.

(i) How many litres are required for production? (1 mark)

[ ] litres

(ii) How many litres must be purchased? (1 mark)

[ ] litres

Calculate overtime hours.

Do not show decimals. Round any decimal figures *up to the next whole number* of hours.

60,000 items of product F are to be delivered in May.

Each one of them takes 3 minutes to produce.

10 staff will each work 200 basic hours.

(c) How many overtime hours must be worked to complete the production? (1 mark)

[ ] hours

(d) Calculate machine utilisation requirements.

Do not show decimals. Round any decimal figures *up to the next whole number* of units. (2 marks)

- There are 8 machines in the department
- Each can be used for 180 hours in the period

Budgeted machine loading	Items	Hours per item	Hours required
Product:			
A	400	1.70	
B	280	1.50	
C	340	0.75	
Total machine hours required			
% utilisation			

(e) Calculate the capacity constraints for product XX by completing the table below. Round down to the maximum whole number in units, if necessary. (5 marks)

According to the standard cost card, each unit of this product requires:

- 5 kg of material
- 1 hour of direct labour time
- 15 minutes of machine time

Budgets have been drafted by the department heads which show:

- Maximum sales demand of 1,000 units
- 10,000 kg of material available
- 800 hours of direct labour time available without using overtime
- 140 hours of machine time available

Production capacity	Units
Sufficient materials are budgeted to manufacture:	
Without overtime, sufficient direct labour is budgeted to manufacture:	
Sufficient machine time is budgeted to manufacture:	
Without overtime, the maximum sales volume is:	
With unlimited overtime, the maximum sales volume is:	

Task 3 (20 marks)

Enter the missing figures in the working schedules and operating budget using the data from the production budget and the notes below.

Production budget	Units
Opening inventory of finished goods	40,000
Production	320,000
Sub-total	360,000
Sales	310,000
Closing inventory of finished goods	50,000

(a) Complete these three working schedules. **(9 marks)**

Materials

Each unit requires 0.75 kg of material.

Closing inventory will be valued at the budgeted purchase price.

Materials	Kg	£
Opening inventory	40,000	50,000
Purchases @ £1.20 per kg		
Subtotal		
Used in production		
Closing inventory	50,000	

Labour

Each item takes 6 minutes to produce.

150 staff work 150 basic hours each in the period.

Overtime is paid at 50% above the basic hourly rate.

Labour	Hours	£
Basic time @ £15 per hour		
Overtime		
Total		

Overhead

Variable overhead is recovered on total labour hours.

Overhead	Hours	£
Variable @ £2.50 per hour		
Fixed		70,750
Total		

Now complete the operating budget.

(b) Enter income, costs and inventories as positive figures.

(6 marks)

Closing finished goods inventory will be valued at the budgeted production cost per unit.

Use a negative figure to indicate a gross loss, for example – 500 or (500).

Use a negative figure to indicate an operating loss, for example – 500 or (500).

Operating budget	Units	£ per unit	£
Sales revenue		£3.50	
Cost of goods sold:			£
Opening inventory of finished goods			120,000
Cost of production		£	
Materials			
Labour			
Overhead			
Closing inventory of finished goods			
Cost of goods sold			
Gross profit			
Overheads		£	
Administration		29,200	
Marketing		30,800	
Operating profit			

(c) Complete the cash flow forecast using the budget data that you have calculated in parts (a) and (b) of this task and the additional information below. (5 marks)

Enter receipts and payments positive figures.

- Receivables will increase by £1,000.
- Materials payables will reduce by £1,400.
- All other payments are made in which they are incurred.
- Production overheads include a depreciation charge of £25,000.

Cash flow forecast	£	£
Opening balance /(overdraft)		1,200,000
Sales receipts		
Payments:		
Material		
Labour		
Production overheads		
Other overheads		
Capital expenditure	50,000	
Total payments		
Closing cash balance/(overdraft)		

Task 4 (20 marks)

You have prepared a draft raw materials budget for the coming year

Background information

- The production budget (units) has already been agreed.
- The production manager and purchasing manager have decided to switch to a new supplier.
- The quality of the material will be improved which should reduce wastage.
- The material price will increase.
- Supply should be more reliable which means that inventory can be reduced.
- You have been asked to recommend performance indicators to monitor material costs and to give advice about ownership of the budget.

Draft raw materials budget	This year actual	Next year budget
Production (units)	64,000	67,840
Material per unit	0.4kg	0.4kg
Material loss (wastage)	12.5%	10%
Material	**kg**	**kg**
Required for production	29,258	30,152
Opening inventory	1,300	1,242
Closing inventory	1,242	1,000
Purchases	29,200	29,910
Material purchases	**£**	**£**
Price per kg	4.80	5.04
Purchases	**140,160**	**150,747**

Write an email to the budget committee, in three sections:

(a) Submit the draft budget for approval and explain the key planning assumptions. (10 marks)

(b) Suggest four appropriate performance indicators (other than cost variances) to monitor raw material costs. (5 marks)

(c) Explain which of the key planning assumptions are based on forecasts and why these are not totally within the production manager's control. (5 marks)

To:	The Budget Committee	**From:**	Budget Accountant
Subject:	**Draft Raw Materials Budget**	**Date:**	xx.xx.xx

(a) Budget submission

(b) Performance indicators

(c) Forecasts

Budget Accountant

Task 5 (20 marks)

(a) Select the appropriate term to match each of these descriptions. **(2 marks)**

Description	Term
A cost that fluctuates in direct proportion to changes in activity	▼
Detailed budgets prepared by functional managers are collated to form a master budget	▼

Picklist:

Bottom up budgeting
Budget flexing
Budget revision
Fixed cost
Incremental budgeting
Rolling budgets
Semi-variable cost
Stepped cost
Top down budgeting
Variable cost
Zero based budgeting

(b) Calculate the sales revenue and cost budgets for April using the budgeted unit data and the information below.

Do not show decimals. Round to the nearest whole number. **(7 marks)**

- Each unit is made from 2 kg of material costing £1.25 per kg.
- It takes three minutes to make each item.
- 650 hours of basic time is available in the month. Any extra hours must be worked in overtime.
- The basic rate is £12 per hour. Overtime is paid at 50% above basic rate.
- Variable overhead relates to labour hours, including overtime.
- Fixed production overhead costs are spread evenly throughout the year.

Budgeted units	Year	April
Units sold	200,000	18,000
Units produced	190,000	17,800

Budget in £	Year	April
Sales revenue	1,100,000	
Cost of sales:		
Material used	475,000	
Direct labour	124,200	
Variable production overhead	60,000	
Fixed production overhead	14,400	
Total production cost	673,600	
Gross profit/(loss)	426,000	

You have submitted a draft operating budget to the budget committee. The committee has asked you to budget for an alternative scenario and calculate the increase or decrease in expected profit.

(c) Complete the alternative scenario column in the operating budget table and calculate the increase or decrease in profit. **(11 marks)**

Assumptions in the first scenario

- Material and labour costs are variable.
- Depreciation is a stepped cost, increasing at every 8,000 units.
- There is an allowance for an energy price rise of 3%.

Alternative scenario

- Increase the selling price by 5%
- Reduce the sales volume by 8%
- Revise the energy price rise to 6%

Apart from sales price per unit, do not enter decimals.

Round to the nearest whole number, if necessary.

Operating budget	First draft	Alternative scenario
Sales price £ per unit	5.00	
Sales volume	110,000	
	£	£
Sales revenue	550,000	
Costs:		
Materials	216,000	
Labour	207,300	
Energy	16,995	
Depreciation	8,400	
Total	448,695	
Gross profit	101,305	
Increase /(decrease) in gross profit		

Task 6 (20 marks)

(a) Select the appropriate term to match the description.

(2 marks)

Description	Term
Budgets prepared for the actual activity level for a period	▼

Picklist:

Bottom up budgeting
Budget flexing
Incremental budgeting
Rolling budgets
Top down budgeting
Zero based budgeting

The operating statement for January showed that direct raw material costs were £277,440. 8,160 kg of material was used and 12,000 units were made and sold. The standard cost allows 0.70 kg of material per unit at a standard price of £33.50 per kg.

(b) Complete the table of direct raw material costs, indicating whether each variance is favourable or adverse. (10 marks)

Direct material costs		Favourable/Adverse
Flexed budget (standard cost)	£	
Actual raw material price per kg (correct to £0.01)	£	
Actual material used per unit (correct to 2dp)	kg	
Price variance	£	▼
Usage variance	£	▼
Cost variance	£	▼
Cost variance % (correct to one decimal place)	%	

(c) Prepare the direct labour cost statement from the activity data provided. (8 marks)

Enter favourable variances as positive figures – for example 500.

Enter adverse variances as negative figures – for example –500.

Activity data	Items produced	Labour hours	Cost (£)
Budget	36,000	576,000	3,456,000
Actual results	34,000	561,000	3,253,800

Direct labour cost statement	£
Standard direct labour cost of production	
Variances (adverse shown as negative)	
Labour rate	
Labour efficiency	
Labour cost	

Task 7 (20 marks)

In this task you are required to complete a monthly operating report. The original budget and actual results have been entered.

You have the following information:

- Material, labour, quality control and distribution costs are variable.
- The costs for energy are semi-variable. The budgeted fixed element is £20,000.
- Equipment hire is a stepped cost, budgeted to increase at every 18,000 units of monthly production
- The budget for marketing costs is stepped, increasing every 10,000 units.
- Depreciation, other production overheads and administration costs are fixed.

Complete the Monthly Operating Report below by flexing the budget, calculating all variances and showing whether each variance is favourable or adverse. (20 marks)

Enter favourable variances as positive figures – for example 500.

Enter adverse variances as negative figures – for example –500.

Monthly Operating Report

Original budget		Flexed budget	Actual	Variance Fav/(Adv)
36,000	Sales volume (units)	35,000	35,000	
£		£	£	£
1,440,000	Sales revenue		1,365,000	
	Costs			
432,000	Material		437,500	
216,000	Labour		203,000	
15,840	Quality control		17,014	
14,400	Distribution		14,970	
92,000	Energy		85,500	
25,000	Equipment hire		25,000	
100,000	Depreciation		70,000	
220,000	Administration		230,000	
37,311	Other production overheads		39,487	
180,000	Marketing		190,000	
1,332,521	Total		1,312,471	
107,479	Operating profit/(Loss)		52,529	

Task 8 (20 marks)

Review the operating statement shown and the additional information below, and prepare a report by email.

Additional information

The budget has been flexed to the actual number of units produced and sold. The original budget was based on an expected sales volume of 165,000 units which was expected to generate a profit of £227,000.

Sales volume reduced when a competitor undercut our prices. We responded with a 10% price reduction partway through the year and expected to win back most of the volume in due course.

The budget allowed for a significant amount of overtime working but this was not required when sales volume fell. Material usage efficiency was better than expected and a budgeted increase in material price did not occur.

The original budget was prepared by a management committee and approved by the Chief Executive. She is concerned that profit is lower than originally budgeted and asks you how she can encourage the management team to perform better.

Operating statement	Flexed budget	Actual	Variance Fav/(Adv)
Sales volume	147,000 units		
	£000	£000	£000
Sales revenue	**764**	**735**	**(29)**
Variable costs			
Material	221	212	9
Labour	125	110	15
Distribution	25	24	1
Power	9	9	–
Equipment hire	138	132	6
Total	518	487	31
Contribution	**246**	**248**	**2**
Fixed costs			
Power	15	14	1
Depreciation	16	17	(1)
Marketing	12	11	1
Administration	7	8	(1)
Total	50	50	–
Operating profit	**196**	**198**	**2**

Write an email to the chief executive, in three sections, in which you explain:

(a) (i) The main reasons for the sales revenue, material and labour variances from the flexed budget.

(ii) How the sales revenue variance might have been avoided. (10 marks)

(b) How to set and manage a budget to drive improved performance. (5 marks)

(c) How the introduction of standard costing could assist effective budgetary control. (5 marks)

To:	The Chief Executive	**From:**	Budget Accountant
Subject:	**Review of Operating Statement**	**Date:**	xx.xx.xx

(a) Reasons for variances

(b) Setting and managing the budget

(c) Standard costing

BPP PRACTICE ASSESSMENT 1 MANAGEMENT ACCOUNTING: BUDGETING

ANSWERS

Management Accounting: Budgeting BPP practice assessment 1

Task 1

(a)

Budget data	Appropriate source
Corporation tax rates	Trade Union
Competitors' financial performance	HM Revenue & Customs
Inflation rates	Financial Times
	Internet search
	Statistics published by Government (eg Office for National Statistics in UK)

(b)

Task	Contact
Obtain details of salaries for proposed new staff	Budget committee
Agree variance reports required for budget	Marketing manager
Draft the direct materials budget	Human resources manager
Obtain details of promotional activity	Trade union representative
	Production manager

(c)

Cost	Accounting treatment
Repairs to head office furniture	Allocate to administration overheads
Water used directly in production	Charge to production in a machine hour overhead rate
Head office extension	Capitalise and depreciate over useful life
Raw material purchases	Direct cost
Production labour – overtime pay	Direct cost
Replacement of head office IT system	Capitalise and depreciate over useful life

(d)

Description	Term
Cost or income data collected over a number of periods, which may be used as a basis for forecasting	Time series

(e)

	Year 1	Year 2	Year 3	Year 4	Year 5
Sales volume index	110.0	117.5	123.6	131.4	140.0
Sales price index	105.0	110.0	115.0	120.0	125.0
	Actual year 1	**Forecast year 2**	**Forecast year 3**	**Forecast year 4**	**Forecast year 5**
At year 1	856,000	914,364	961,833	1,022,531	1,089,455
At expected prices		957,905	1,053,436	1,168,607	1,296,970

Forecast sales at year 1 prices:

Year 2 £856,000 × (117.5/110.0) = £914,364
Year 3 £856,000 × (123.6/110.0) = £961,833
Year 4 £856,000 × (131.4/110.0) = £1,022,531
Year 5 £856,000 × (140.0/110.0) = £1,089,455

Forecast sales at expected prices:

Year 2 £914,364 × (110.0/105.0) = £957,905
Year 3 £961,833 × (115.0/105.0) = £1,053,436
Year 4 £1,022,531 × (120.0/105.0) = £1,168,607
Year 5 £1,089,455 × (125.0/105.0) = £1,296,970

Task 2

(a)

Production (units)	Week 1	Week 2	Week 3	Week 4	Week 5
Sales volume	500	550	600	650	700
Opening inventory	100	69	75	82	
Closing inventory	69	75	82	88	
Saleable production	469	556	607	656	
Rejected production	100	118	129	140	
Total manufactured units	569	674	736	796	

You are given the opening inventory figure, so can calculate the closing and opening inventory figures for the rest of the five weeks. From this, with sales, you can calculate the saleable production figures (sales + closing inventory – opening inventory = saleable production). You can then calculate the figures for rejected production and for total manufactured units.

(b) (i) How many litres are required for production?

14,836 litres

(ii) How many litres must be purchased?

14,936 litres

Working	
Units manufactured	900
× 15 litres each	13,500
÷ 91% = total litres required	14,836
Opening inventory	(500)
Closing inventory	600
Total manufactured units	14,936

(c) The correct answer is:

1,000	hours

Workings

60,000 items × 3 minutes each = 180,000 minutes of labour required

180,000 minutes ÷ 60 = 3,000 hours of labour required

200 × 10 = 2,000 basic hours available

3,000 – 2,000 = 1,000 hours overtime required

(d)

Budgeted machine loading	Items	Hours per item	Hours required
Product:			
A	400	1.70	680
B	280	1.50	420
C	340	0.75	255
Total machine hours required			1,355
% utilisation 1,355 / (8 × 180)			94%

(e)

Production capacity	Units
Sufficient materials are budgeted to manufacture: (10,000/7)	2,000
Without overtime, sufficient direct labour is budgeted to manufacture: (800/1)	800
Sufficient machine time is budgeted to manufacture: (140/0.25)	560
Without overtime, the maximum sales volume is:	560*
With unlimited overtime, the maximum sales volume is:	560*

*Cannot be higher than maximum units from budgeted machine time

Task 3

(a)

Materials	Kg	£
Opening inventory	40,000	50,000
Purchases @ £1.20 per kg	250,000	300,000
Subtotal	290,000	350,000
Used in production	240,000 (W1)	290,000
Closing inventory	50,000	60,000 (W2)

Workings

1 Production materials = 320,000 × 0.75 = 240,000
2 Closing inventory = 50,000 × 300,000/250,000

Labour	Hours	£
Basic time @ £15 per hour	22,500 (W3)	337,500
Overtime	9,500	213,750 (W5)
Total	32,000 (W4)	551,250

Workings

3 Basic hours = 150 staff × 150 hours = 22,500
4 Total labour required = 320,000 ÷ 10 = 32,000 hours
5 Overtime = 9,500 × £15 × 1.5

Overhead	Hours	£
Variable @ £2.50 per hour	32,000	80,000
Fixed		70,750
Total		150,750

(b)

Operating budget	Units	£ per unit	£
Sales revenue	310,000	£3.50	1,085,000
Cost of goods sold:			
Opening inventory of finished goods (40,000 units)			120,000
Cost of production		**£**	
Materials		290,000	
Labour		551,250	
Overhead		150,750	992,000
Closing inventory of finished goods			155,000
Cost of goods sold			957,000
Gross profit			128,000
Overheads		**£**	
Administration		29,200	
Marketing		30,800	60,000
Operating profit			68,000

Working

Closing inventory of finished goods

Budgeted production cost per unit is £992,000 ÷ 320,000 units = £3.10/unit.

Hence closing inventory of finished goods is valued at 50,000 units × £3.10 = £155,000.

(c)

Cash flow forecast	£	£
Opening balance / (overdraft)		1,200,000
Sales receipts		1,084,000
Payments:		
Material	301,400	
Labour	551,250	
Production overheads	125,750	
Other overheads	60,000	
Capital expenditure	50,000	
Total payments		1,088,400
Closing cash balance/(overdraft)		1,195,600

Workings

Sales receipts: £1,085,000 – £1,000 = £1,084,000

Material purchases: £300,000 + £1,400 = £301,400

Production overhead: £150,750 – £25,000 = £125,750

Task 4

(a) Budget submission

I attach the proposed raw materials budget for next year for your consideration and approval. This year's results are shown for comparison.

This draft is based on the agreed production budget of 67,840 units which is 6% more than this year. However, the quantity of raw material purchases should increase by only 3.1%.

The material required in each unit of production will be unchanged at 0.4 kg. However, the production manager expects to reduce material from a more reliable supplier.

The purchasing manager supports this strategy but expects material price to rise by 5%.

Overall the material purchases budget shows an increase of 7.6%, compared with this year.

(b) Performance indicators

A number of assumptions have been made in this budget and we need to monitor their achievement.

I recommend that we review the following four indicators on a weekly basis.

- Material usage per unit of production
- Percentage of material wastage
- Price per kilo
- Number of days of material inventory

(c) Forecasts

Although the production manager should take ownership of this budget there are aspects of it which are not wholly within his/her control.

Purchase prices will be negotiated by the purchasing manager. The two managers need to work together to balance quality with price.

Wastage is an important factor and is at least partly dependent upon quality. The wastage level has been estimated for budget purposes and must be monitored carefully.

A reduction in inventory is planned. This will only be possible if the supplier proves to be more reliable, as anticipated.

Finally, the production manager cannot control production demand, although allowance for this can be made with budget flexing.

Task 5

(a)

Description	Term
A cost that fluctuates in direct proportion to changes in activity	Variable cost
Detailed budgets prepared by functional managers are collated to form a master budget	Bottom up budgeting

(b)

Budgeted units	Year	April
Units sold	200,000	18,000
Units produced	190,000	17,800

Budget in £	Year	April
Sales revenue	1,100,000	99,000 (W1)
Cost of sales:		
Material used	475,000	44,500 (W2)
Direct labour	124,200	12,120 (W3)
Variable production overhead	60,000	5,621 (W4)
Fixed production overhead	14,400	1,200
Total production cost	673,600	63,441
Gross profit/(loss)	426,000	35,559

Workings

1 Price = £1,100,000 ÷ 200,000 = £5.50/unit

£5.50 × 18,000 units = £99,000

2 17,800 units × 2kg × £1.25/kg = £44,500

3 Labour hours required = 17,800 units × 3 minutes ÷ 60mins/hour = 890 hours

650 hours @ £12/hr = £7,800

240 hours @ £12/hr × 1.5 = £4,320

Total = £7,800 + £4,320 = £12,120

4 Variable production overhead for April = £60,000 × 890 hours / total annual labour hours

Total annual labour hours = 190,000 × 3 ÷ 60 = 9,500 hours

Hence £60,000 × 890/9500 = £5,621

(c)

Operating budget	First draft	Alternative scenario	Working
Sales price £ per unit	5.00	5.25	5 × 1.05
Sales volume	110,000	101,200	110,000 × 0.92
	£	£	
Sales revenue	550,000	531,300	5.25 × 101,200
Costs:			
Materials	216,000	198,720	216,000 × 0.92
Labour	207,300	190,716	207,300 × 0.92
Energy	16,995	17,490	16,995/1.03 × 1.06
Depreciation	8,400	7,800	W1
Total	448,695	414,726	
Gross profit	101,305	116,574	
Increase/(decrease) in gross profit		15,269	

Working

Depreciation is in steps of 8,000 by volume. Therefore the charge at volume of 110,000 puts this at the 14th step. Each step is therefore £8,400/14 = £600.

A volume of 101,200 ÷ 8,000 = 12.65, ie the 13th step. £600 × 13 = £7,800.

Task 6

(a)

Description	Term
Budgets prepared for the actual activity level for a period	Budget flexing

(b)

Direct material costs		Favourable/Adverse
Flexed budget (standard cost)	£281,400 W1	
Actual raw material price per kg (correct to £0.01)	£34.00 W2	
Actual material used per unit (correct to 2dp)	0.68 kg W3	
Price variance	£4,080 W4	Adverse
Usage variance	£8,040 W5	Favourable
Cost variance	£3,960 W6	Favourable
Cost variance % (correct to one decimal place)	1.4% W7	

Workings

1 No of units produced × standard usage × standard price = 12,000 × 0.70 × 33.50 = £281,400

2 Total material cost/total material used = 277,440/8,160 = £34.00

3 Total material used/no of units produced = 8,160/12,000 = 0.68 kg

4 (Standard price – actual price) × material used = (33.50 – 34.00) × 8,160 = –£4,080

5 (Standard usage – actual usage) × std price × actual units (0.70 – 0.68) × 33.50 × 12,000 = £8,040

6 Flexed budget cost – actual cost = £281,400 – £277,440 = £3,960

7 Cost variance/flexed budget cost = 3,960/281,400 = 1.4%

(c)

Direct labour cost statement	£
Standard direct labour cost of production	3,264,000 *W1*
Variances (adverse shown as negative)	
Labour rate	112,200 *W2*
Labour efficiency	–102,000 *W3*
Labour cost	10,200

Workings

1 3,456,000 ÷ 36,000 = £96

£96 × 34,000 = £3,264,000

2 Standard rate = 3,456,000 ÷ 576,000 = £6.00/hr

Actual rate = 3,253,800 ÷ 561,000 = £5.80/hr

Labour rate variance = (£6 – £5.80) × 561,000 = £112,200

Variance is favourable – actual rate is lower than budget.

3 Standard efficiency = 576,000 ÷ 36,000 = 16hrs/unit

Actual efficiency = 561,000 ÷ 34,000 = 16.5hrs/unit

Labour efficiency variance = (16 – 16.5) × £6/hr × 34,000 = –£102,000

Variance is adverse – actual efficiency is worse than budget (more hours per unit).

Task 7

Original budget		Flexed budget	Actual	Variance Fav/(Adv)
36,000	Sales volume (units)	35,000	35,000	
£		£	£	£
1,440,000	Sales revenue (W1)	1,400,000	1,365,000	–35,000
	Costs			
432,000	Material (W2)	420,000	437,500	–17,500
216,000	Labour (W3)	210,000	203,000	7,000
15,840	Quality control (W4)	15,400	17,014	–1,614
14,400	Distribution (W5)	14,000	14,970	–970
92,000	Energy (W6)	90,000	85,500	4,500
25,000	Equipment hire (W7)	25,000	25,000	0
100,000	Depreciation	100,000	70,000	30,000
220,000	Administration	220,000	230,000	–10,000
37,311	Other production overheads	37,311	39,487	–2,176

Original budget		Flexed budget	Actual	Variance Fav/(Adv)
180,000	Marketing (W8)	180,000	190,000	–10,000
1,332,521	Total	1,311,711	1,312,471	–760
107,479	Operating profit/(Loss)	88,289	52,529	–35,760

Workings

1 Budgeted selling price per unit

Revenue (turnover)/sales volume

£1,440,000/36,000 = £40

Flexed budget: 35,000 × £40 = £1,400,000

2 Budgeted material cost

£432,000/36,000 = £12

Flexed budget: 35,000 × £12 = £420,000

3 Budgeted labour cost

£216,000/36,000 = £6

Flexed budget: 35,000 × £6 = £210,000

4 Quality control cost

£15,840/36,000 = £0.44

Flexed budget: 35,000 × £0.44 = £15,400

5 Distribution cost

£14,400/36,000 = £0.40

Flexed budget: 35,000 × £0.40 = £14,000

6 Budgeted energy cost.

Fixed element = £20,000

Original budget, variable element = £92,000 – £20,000 = £72,000

Variable element per unit = £72,000/36,000 = £2 per unit

Flexed budget variable element 35,000 × £2 = £70,000

Total flexed cost = £20,000 + £70,000 = £90,000

7 Equipment is in steps of 18,000 by volume. Therefore the charge at volume of 36,000 puts this at the 2nd step. Each step is therefore £25,000 ÷ 2 = £12,500.

A volume of 35,000 ÷ 18,000 = 1.94, ie the 2nd step. £12,500 × 2 = £25,000.

8 Budgeted marketing cost is stepped, but original and flexed budget in the same range so flexed budget = £180,000.

Task 8

(a) Reasons for variances

I have reviewed the results for the period. There was an operating profit of £198,000 compared with the flexed budget profit of £196,000. The original budget anticipated a profit of £227,000 based on sales of 165,000 units.

Compared with the original budget, the result is disappointing and this is attributed to a loss of sales volume due to price competition. The volume was 11% below the original budget despite our own 10% price reduction during the year. The flexed budget calculations indicate that lost sales should have generated a profit of £31,000 (£227,000 less £196,000). The flexed budget is based on the original but with appropriate volume adjustments.

The unforeseen competition has taken sales volume from us and forced us to make 10% price reductions. The full year impact of the price reduction is significant and we are not confident that volume will recover fully. This situation might have been avoided with better market intelligence and a proactive marketing campaign.

Compared with the flexed budget there was an adverse sales variance of £29,000 (3.8%), caused by the 10% price reduction part way through the year.

However, there was a £9,000 favourable variance on material costs (4%) where both material price and usage were lower than budgeted. Similarly, the labour cost variance was £15,000 favourable (12%). With production volumes less than budgeted there was less need to work overtime at premium rate.

(b) Setting and managing the budget

To be challenging, budgets should be stretching, always striving for improvement, whilst being achievable. We can see from the operating statement that the adverse sales variance was counterbalanced by unrelated and fortuitous favourable cost variances in materials and labour. It can be argued that the budget was poorly focused, failing to address the threat of competition and not challenging managers to improve efficiency.

I recommend that we introduce closer scrutiny at the budget setting stage to ensure that budgetary slack is not permitted and that efficiency improvements are planned and introduced. A stretching budget is likely to motivate managers to improve performance. Variances need to be fully analysed and explained on a regular basis and corrective action taken promptly.

(c) Standard costing

Standard costing is an effective mechanism for bringing rigour to budgetary control. It makes sense to set standards for production resources at the level of a single unit of production. The standards can be multiplied by planned production levels to create cost budgets.

The system facilitates the calculation of detailed cost variances which helps managers to understand and manage the resources effectively. Looking at the operating statement, for example, we could analyse the material variance into the price and efficiency aspects and also see whether the labour variance was wholly due to saved overtime premium.

BPP PRACTICE ASSESSMENT 2 MANAGEMENT ACCOUNTING: BUDGETING

Time allowed: 2.5 hours

PRACTICE ASSESSMENT 2

Management Accounting: Budgeting BPP practice assessment 2

Task 1 (20 marks)

A factory has two production departments, assembly and finishing.

(a) Match the factory overheads (on the left) with the most appropriate method of attributing these overheads between the two departments. (3 marks)

(CBT instructions: Click on a box in the left column, then on one in the right column. To remove a line, click on it.)

Overheads
Rent and rates
Canteen expenses
Inventory insurance

Method of allocation
Number of staff employed
Floor area
Units produced
Average inventory held

(b) As budget accountant, match each task with the person or group that you will need to contact. (4 marks)

(CBT instructions: Click on a box in the left column, then on one in the right column. To remove a line, click on it.)

Task
Draft the direct labour budget
Obtain details of machinery to be purchased in the coming year
Obtain details of staff redundancies
Agree deadlines for production of budgets

Contact
Budget committee
Marketing manager
Human resources manager
Trade union representative
Production manager

(c) Drag each item below and drop it into its appropriate budget. (6 marks)

- Legal fees regarding late payment by customers
- Advertising costs
- Cost of new computer system for office
- Depreciation costs of new computer system
- Cost of annual audit
- Wastage costs incurred on production line
- Cost of factory supervisors

Classification	Expenditure
Labour	
Material	
Sales and marketing	
Administration	
Capital	
Human resources	

(d) Select the appropriate term to match each of these descriptions. (1 mark)

Description	Term
A method of costing which allocates overheads to cost units by considering the activities that cause the overhead to be incurred and the factors that give rise to the costs (cost drivers)	▼

Picklist:

Absorption costing
Activity based costing
Cost driver
Variable or marginal costing

The budget committee has set the sales volume growth and pricing assumptions for years 2, 3, 4 and 5 in the form of indices.

(e) Complete the sales revenue forecast below. Do not show decimals. Round up each figure *to the nearest whole number.*
(6 marks)

	Year 1	Year 2	Year 3	Year 4	Year 5
Sales volume index	120.0	121.2	125.7	126.9	130.0
Sales price index	117.2	119.7	121.0	123.4	126.7
	Actual year 1	**Forecast year 2**	**Forecast year 3**	**Forecast year 4**	**Forecast year 5**
At year 1 prices	56,300				
At expected prices					

Task 2 (20 marks)

(a) Complete the following production forecast for product J based on the information below. Do not show decimals. Round any decimal figures *up to the next whole number* of units.
(10 marks)

Closing inventory is expected to be 10% more than opening inventory for each month.

Production (units)	July	August	September
Sales	1,000	1,000	1,000
Opening inventory	500		
Closing inventory			
Production			

(b) Calculate production and inventory levels.

Do not show decimals. Round any decimal figures *up to the next whole number* of litres.

50 workers are each expected to work 1,800 hours a year basic time.

10% of this time is idle time.

Each unit requires 15 minutes of labour time

3% of units are rejected as defective.

The opening inventory will be 50,263 units.

How many non-defective units will be produced? (1 mark)

[ ] units

How many units will be in inventory at the end of the period? (1 mark)

[ ] units

(c) Calculate materials usage.

The sales budget is for 200,000 units in the period.

Each unit requires 3 kg of material.

The opening inventory is 18,000 units.

The closing inventory is 35,000 units.

What is the materials usage budget? [ ] kg

(1 mark)

(d) Calculate materials usage.

Product A contains 5 kg of material X.

1,000 units of product A are to be produced.

Product B contains 2 kg of material X.

2,000 units of product B are to be produced.

Product C contains 1 kg of material X.

500 units of product C are to be produced.

The production process for each product wastes 2% of material.

What is the materials usage budget (rounded to the nearest kg)? (2 marks)

[ ] kg

(e) Calculate sub-contracting requirements.

Do not show decimals. Round any decimal figures *up to the next whole number* of units.

8,000 items of product R, are to be manufactured next week.

Each one takes 3 minutes to produce.

320 production labour hours are available.

Any additional requirement must be sub-contracted.

How many units must be sub-contracted? (5 marks)

[ ] units

Task 3 (20 marks)

Enter the missing figures in the working schedules and operating budget using the data from the production budget and the notes below.

Production budget	Units
Opening inventory of finished goods	5,000
Production	42,000
Sub-total	47,000
Sales	44,000
Closing inventory of finished goods	3,000

(a) Complete these three working schedules. **(9 marks)**

Materials

Each unit produced requires 1.2 kg of material.

Closing inventory will be valued at the budgeted purchase price.

Materials	Kg	£
Opening inventory	7,200	10,080
Purchases @ £1.50 per kg		
Sub-total		
Used in production		
Closing inventory	6,000	

Labour

It takes 6 minutes to make each item.

22 staff work 180 basic hours each.

Overtime is paid at 40% above the basic hourly rate.

Labour	Hours	£
Basic time @ £12 per hour		
Overtime		
Total		

Overhead

Variable overhead is recovered on total labour hours.

Overhead	Hours	£
Variable @ £1.10 per hour		
Fixed		3,348
Total		

Now complete the operating budget.

(b) Enter income, costs and inventories as positive figures.

(6 marks)

Closing inventory will be valued at the budgeted total cost of production per unit.

Use a negative figure to indicate a gross loss, for example –500 or (500).

Use a negative figure to indicate an operating loss, for example –500 or (500).

Operating budget	Units	£ per unit	£
Sales revenue		4.20	
Cost of goods sold:			
Opening inventory of finished goods			15,000
Cost of production		£	
Materials			
Labour			
Production overhead			
Closing inventory of finished goods			
Cost of goods sold			
Gross profit			
Overheads:		£	
Administration		1,500	
Marketing		2,100	
Operating profit			

(c) Complete the cash flow forecast using the budget data that you have calculated in parts (a) and (b) of this task and the additional information below.

Enter receipts and payments positive figures and round *up to the nearest whole number.* **(5 marks)**

- Receivables will decrease by £5,000.
- Materials payables will increase by £5,300.
- Labour are paid one month in arrears. This month's labour cost is 2% higher than that of the previous month.
- All other payments are made in the period in which they are incurred.
- An item of machinery will be acquired at a cost of £80,000. This will be paid for in instalments; the first payment is made this month for 25% of the full cost.

Cash flow forecast	£	£
Opening balance / (overdraft)		(56,567)
Sales receipts		
Payments:		
Materials		
Labour		
Production overheads		
Capital expenditure		
Total payments		
Closing cash balance/(overdraft)		

Task 4 (20 marks)

You have prepared a draft direct labour budget for the coming year.

Background information

An organisation provides training for students wishing to pass professional examinations. The organisation offers a 'guaranteed pass' scheme, to which the following data relates.

Data collected includes:

- Number of courses
- Number of students
- Number of qualifications awarded

	This year actual	Next year budget
Number of courses	2,567	2,465
Number of students	56,474	58,062
Number of qualifications awarded	9,412	9,677
Labour hours per qualification awarded	87	83
Labour		
Required for production (hours)	818,844	803,191
Labour hours @ Standard rate	750,000	750,000
Labour cost @ Standard rate (£20/hour)	£15,000,000	£15,000,000
Labour hours @ Overtime rate	68,844	53,191
Labour cost @ Overtime rate (£30/hour)	£2,065,320	£1,595,730
Direct labour cost total (£)	**£17,065,320**	**£16,595,730**

Write an e-mail to the budget committee, in two parts:

(a) Requesting approval for the budget and explaining the assumptions upon which it is based. (10 marks)

(b) Recommending four performance indicators that could be used to measure the quality of the organisation's service, against budget. You are not restricted to using only the data listed above. (10 marks)

To:	Budget committee	**Date:**	xx.xx.xx
From:	An Accounting Technician	**Subject:**	Performance indicators for quality

(a) Budget submission

(b) Performance indicators for quality

Task 5 (20 marks)

(a) Select the appropriate term to match the description.

(2 marks)

Description	Term
Senior management prepare a master budget and delegate the responsibility for producing departmental budgets	▼
A cost which has both a fixed element and a variable element	▼

Picklist:

Bottom up budgeting
Fixed
Incremental budgeting
Rolling Budgets
Semi-variable
Stepped
Top down budgeting
Variable
Zero base budgeting

(b) Calculate the sales revenue and cost budgets for January using the budgeted unit data and the information below.

Do not show decimals. Round up to the nearest whole number.

(7 marks)

- Material costs are variable.
- The company has 25 workers working equal basic hours each month, totalling 2,000 per worker in the year.
- Labour costs £9 per hour basic time. Overtime is paid at £11 per hour.
- Each unit requires 0.5 hours of labour.
- Administrative costs are incurred evenly through the year.

Budgeted units	Year	January
Units sold	100,000	8,333
Units produced	105,000	9,000

Budget in £	Year	January
Sales revenue	5,000,000	
Material used	472,500	
Direct labour	477,500	
Administrative expenditure	24,000	

You have submitted a draft operating budget to the budget committee. The committee has asked you to budget for an alternative scenario and calculate the increase or decrease in expected profit.

(c) Complete the alternative scenario column in the operating budget table and calculate the increase or decrease in profit. **(11 marks)**

Assumptions in the first scenario

Material and labour costs are variable.

Depreciation is a stepped cost, increasing at every 6,500 units.

There is an allowance for a water price rise of 4%.

Alternative scenario

Increase the selling price by 9%.

Reduce the sales volume by 9%.

Revise the water price rise to 5%.

Apart from sales price per unit, do not enter decimals.

***Round to the nearest whole number*, if necessary.**

Operating budget	First draft	Alternative scenario
Sales price £ per unit	6.00	
Sales volume	90,000	
	£	£
Sales revenue	540,000	
Costs:		
Materials	190,000	
Labour	150,500	
Water	16,666	
Depreciation	7,000	
Total	364,166	
Gross profit	175,834	
Increase/(decrease) in gross profit		

Task 6 (20 marks)

(a) Select the appropriate term to match the description.

(2 marks)

Description	Term
A financial measure of the difference between budget and actual performance	▼

Picklist:

Labour efficiency variance
Labour rate variance
Material usage variance
Performance indicator
Variance
Variance analysis

The operating statement for June showed that direct labour costs were £65,309. 3,500 labour hours were used and 8,000 units were made and sold. The standard cost allows 0.5 hrs of labour time per unit at a standard price of £18.00 per hour.

(b) Complete the table of direct labour costs, indicating whether each variance is favourable or adverse. (10 marks)

Direct labour costs		Favourable/ Adverse
Flexed budget (standard cost)	£	
Actual labour cost per hour (correct to £0.01)	£	
Actual labour hours per unit (correct to 2dp)	hrs	
Rate variance	£	▼
Efficiency variance	£	▼
Cost variance	£	▼
Cost variance % (correct to one decimal place)	%	

Picklist:

Adverse
Favourable

(c) Prepare the direct materials cost statement from the activity data provided. (8 marks)

Enter favourable variances as positive figures – for example 500.

Enter adverse variances as negative figures – for example –500.

Activity data	Items produced	Materials used (kg)	Cost (£)
Budget	2,000	44,000	880,000
Actual results	2,420	45,980	827,640

Direct materials cost statement	£
Standard direct materials cost of production	
Variances (adverse shown as negative)	
Materials price	
Materials usage	
Materials cost	

Task 7 (20 marks)

The budgeted and actual performance for a month is given below.

Flex the budget to the actual activity level, given the information below about costs, and show whether each variance is favourable or adverse. (20 marks)

Enter favourable variances as positive figures – for example 500.

Enter adverse variances as negative figures – for example –500.

Operating budget		Flexed budget	Actual	Variance Fav/(Adv)
120,000	Sales volume (units)	140,000	140,000	
£		£	£	£
6,000,000	Sales revenue		6,720,000	
	Costs			
1,080,000	Material		1,313,680	
660,000	Labour		782,310	
150,000	Production managers		192,000	
24,000	Distribution		35,281	
250,000	Energy		296,530	
30,000	Equipment hire		30,000	
414,000	Depreciation		412,000	

Operating budget		Flexed budget	Actual	Variance Fav/(Adv)
332,000	Marketing and advertising		315,320	
529,000	Administration		534,200	
202,000	Other production overheads		212,300	
3,671,000	Total costs		4,123,621	
2,329,000	Operating profit		2,596,379	

Material, labour and distribution costs are variable.

Energy cost is semi-variable. The variable element is budgeted at £1.50 per unit of sales.

Production managers are a stepped cost. For health and safety reasons, there must always be at least two production managers for each production line in operation. Each production line has a maximum output of 45,000 units per month and only the minimum number of production lines are operated each month.

Production overheads included a fixed element of £100,000.

Equipment hire is a stepped cost, increasing for every 50,000 units of production.

Depreciation, marketing and advertising, and administration costs are fixed.

You are required to flex the budget, calculate variances and show whether each variance is favourable or adverse. The actual results have been entered for you.

Task 8 (20 marks)

Review the operating statement shown and the additional information below, and prepare a report by email.

Additional information

The business manufactures chocolates.

During the period, the world's largest supplier of the raw material, cocoa, purchased a competitor and was able to push prices upwards given its large market share. The business switched suppliers several times, but this led to quality issues.

During the summer, one of the two machines for production broke down. This led to the machine being out of service for two weeks while a specialist carried out extensive repairs.

Following the decision to stop giving inventory away free to staff, the workforce slowed their production for three weeks until management reversed its decision.

Operating statement	Flexed budget £	Actual £	Variance Fav/(Adverse) £
Sales revenue	12,400,000	11,000,000	(1,400,000)
Material	(2,550,000)	(4,012,500)	(1,462,500)
Labour	(5,350,000)	(5,800,000)	(450,000)
Variable production overheads	(1,070,000)	(1,085,000)	(15,000)
Fixed production overheads	(535,000)	(791,250)	(256,250)
Profit/(loss)	2,895,000	(688,750)	(3,583,750)

Write an email to the Managing Director in which you:

(a) Suggest possible reasons for the variances on materials, labour, fixed production overheads and sales. (10 marks)

(b) Explain actions that should be taken in relation to setting the following year's budget, in the light of these variances. (10 marks)

To:	Managing Director	**Date:**	(Today)
From:	Budget Accountant	**Subject:**	**Reasons for variances and actions**

Reasons for variances

Actions

BPP PRACTICE ASSESSMENT 2 MANAGEMENT ACCOUNTING: BUDGETING

ANSWERS

Management Accounting: Budgeting BPP practice assessment 2

Task 1

(a)

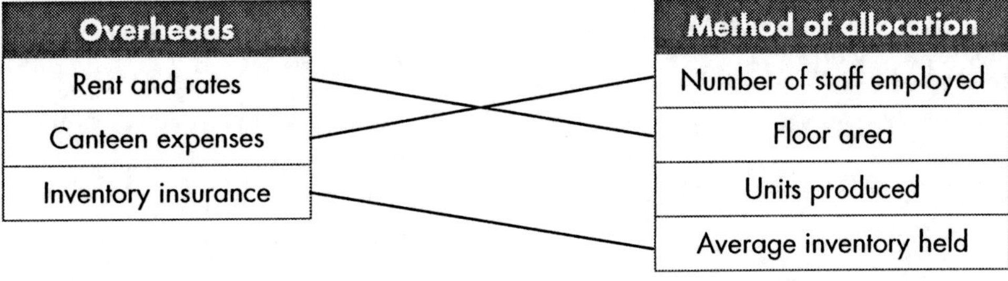

(b)

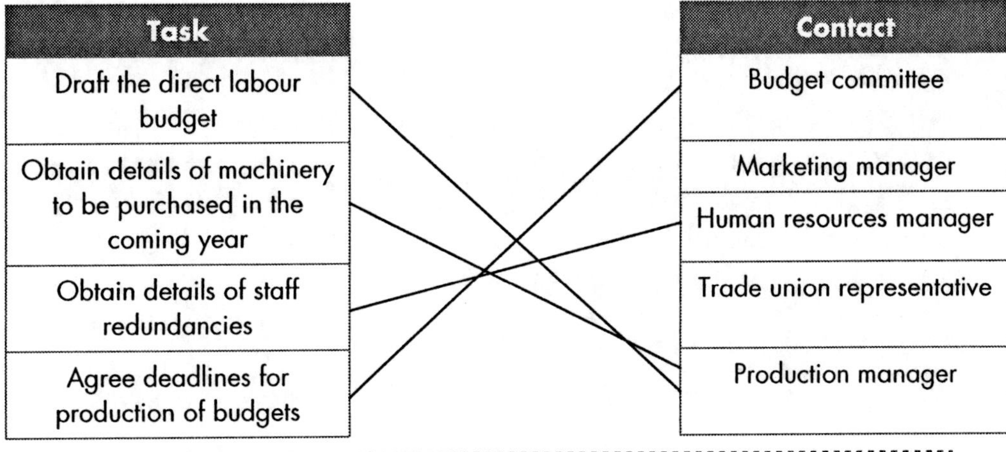

(c)

Classification	Expenditure
Labour	Cost of factory supervisors
Material	Wastage costs incurred on production line
Sales and marketing	Advertising costs
Administration	Legal fees regarding late payment by customers Depreciation costs of new computer system Cost of annual audit
Capital	Cost of new computer system for office
Human resources	Cost of recruitment agency fees

(d)

Description	Term
A method of costing which allocates overheads to cost units by considering the activities that cause the overhead to be incurred and the factors that give rise to the costs (cost drivers)	Activity based costing

(e)

	Year 1	Year 2	Year 3	Year 4	Year 5
Sales volume index	120.0	121.2	125.7	126.9	130.0
Sales price index	117.2	119.7	121.0	123.4	126.7
	Actual year 1	**Forecast year 2**	**Forecast year 3**	**Forecast year 4**	**Forecast year 5**
At year 1 prices	56,300	56,863	58,975	59,538	60,992
At expected prices		58,076	60,886	62,688	65,936

Forecast sales at year 1 prices:

Year 2 £56,300 × (121.2/120.0) = £56,863
Year 3 £56,300 × (125.7/120.0) = £58,975
Year 4 £56,300 × (126.9/120.0) = £59,538
Year 5 £56,300 × (130.0/120.0) = £60,992

Forecast sales at expected prices:

Year 2 £56,863 × (119.7/117.2) = £58,076
Year 3 £58,975 × (121.0/117.2) = £60,888
Year 4 £59,538 × (123.4/117.2) = £62,688
Year 5 £60,992 × (126.7/117.2) = £65,936

Task 2

(a)

	July	August	September
Sales	1,000	1,000	1,000
Opening inventory	500	550	605
Closing inventory	550	605	666
Production	1,050	1,055	1,061

(b)

The correct answers are: | 314,280 | units and | 364,543 | units

Working

Hours worked = 50 × 1,800 = 90,000

Productive hours = 90,000 × 90% = 81,000 hours

Hours per unit = 0.25

Units produced = 81,000/0.25 = 324,000

Non-defective units produced = 97% × 324,000 = 314,280

Opening inventory = 50,263

Closing inventory = 50,263 + 314,280 = 364,543

(c)

The materials usage budget is | 651,000 | kg

Working

Production budget = sales + closing inventory – opening inventory = 200,000 + 35,000 – 18,000 = 217,000 units.

Materials usage = 217,000 × 3 kg = 651,000 kg

(d)

The materials usage budget in kg is | 9,649 |

Working

Material required:

Product A: 5 kg × 1,000 = 5,000 kg

Product B: 2 kg × 2,000 = 4,000 kg

Product C: 1 kg × 500 = 500 kg

Total = 9,500 kg

Total including wastage = 9,500 × 100/98 = 9,694 kg

(e)

The correct answer is: 1,600 units

8,000 items × 3 minutes = 24,000 minutes

24,000 minutes ÷ 60 = 400 hours needed

400 hours needed – 320 hours available = 80 hours to be sub-contracted

80 hours × 60 = 4,800 minutes to be sub-contracted

4,800 minutes ÷ 3 = 1,600 units to be sub-contracted

Task 3

(a)

Materials	kg	£
Opening inventory	7,200	10,080
Purchases @ £1.50 per kg	49,200	73,800
Sub-total	56,400	83,880
Used in production	50,400	74,880
Closing inventory	6,000	9,000

Working

42,000 × 1.2 kg = 50,400 kg will be used in production

Closing inventory = 6,000, therefore Opening inventory + Purchases = 50,400 + 6000 = 56,400

Purchases = 56,400 – 7,200

Closing inventory is valued at budgeted purchase price of £1.50 per kg, that is at £9,000.

Labour	Hours	£
Basic time @ £12 per hour	3,960	47,520
Overtime	240	4,032
Total	4,200	51,552

Working

42,000 × 6/60 = 4,200 labour hours are required in total but only 22 × 180 = 3,960 basic hours are available, so 4,200 – 3,960 = 240 hours must be paid at overtime rates: 240 × £12 × 1.4 = £4,032.

Overhead	Hours	£
Variable @ £1.10 per hour	4,200	4,620
Fixed		3,348
Total		7,968

(b)

Operating budget	Units	£ per unit	£
Sales revenue	44,000	4.20	184,800
Cost of goods sold:			
Opening inventory of finished goods			15,000
Cost of production		£	
Materials		74,880	
Labour		51,552	
Production overhead		7,968	134,400
Closing inventory of finished goods (134,400/42,000 × 3,000)			9,600
Cost of goods sold			139,800
Gross profit			45,000
Overheads:		£	
Administration		1,500	
Marketing		2,100	3,600
Operating profit			41,400

(c)

Cash flow forecast	£	£
Opening balance / (overdraft)		(56,567)
Sales receipts		189,800
Payments:		
Materials	68,500	
Labour	50,542	
Production overheads	7,968	
Capital expenditure	20,000	
Total payments		147,010
Closing cash balance/(overdraft)		(13,777)

W1: Sales receipts = Revenue – change in receivables = 184,800 – (–5,000) = £189,800

W2: Materials payments = Material cost – change in payables = 73,800 – 5,300 = £68,500

W3: Labour payments = Labour cost this month ÷ 1.02 = 51,552 ÷ 1.02 = £50,542

W4: Capital expenditure = 80,000 × 25% = £20,000

Task 4

To: Budget committee **Date:** xx.xx.xx

From: An Accounting Technician **Subject:** **Performance indicators for quality**

(a) Budget submission

I attach the proposed labour budget for next year for your consideration and approval. This year's results are shown for comparison.

This draft is based on the agreed number of 2,465 courses, which is 4% fewer than this year. The total number of labour hours is expected to fall from 818,844 to 803,191, which is 1.9%.

The number of labour hours worked at the standard rate will remain constant at 750,000 hours. The fall in the total labour hours needed will result in a fall in overtime hours from 68,844 hours to 53,191 hours. Overtime payments will fall by £469,590.

Overall the direct labour budget shows a reduction of 2.8% compared with this year. However, the number of qualifications awarded is set to rise by 2.8%, which should result in increased revenue being recognised during the year.

(b) Performance indicators for quality

A number of different indicators can help assess quality. Standards or targets must be set and then the actual performance compared against these.

Many quantitative indicators are given below. However, as the quality of service will also be judged by the students ie the customers, I recommend surveys are undertaken at the end of each course to obtain feedback about the quality of service from the students.

Non-financial quantitative indicators:

Percentage of students awarded a qualification

Number of individual exam passes

Number of first time passes per number of exams taken

Pass rates per course

Number of complaints from students

Average marks obtained compared with average for that exam nationwide

Tutorial note: only four indicators are required.

Task 5

(a)

Description	Term
Senior management prepare a master budget and delegate the responsibility for producing departmental budgets	Top down budgeting
A cost which has both a fixed element and a variable element	Semi-variable

(b)

Budgeted units	Year	January
Units sold	100,000	8,333
Units produced	105,000	9,000

	Year	January
Sales revenue	5,000,000	416,650 W1
Material used	472,500	40,500 W2
Direct labour	477,500	41,166 W3
Administrative expenditure	24,000	2,000

Workings

1 Sales price per unit = £5,000,000/100,000 = £50
January sales = 8,333 × £50 = £416,650

2 Material
Price per unit = £472,500/105,000 = £4.50 per unit
January materials usage = £4.50 × 9,000 = £40,500

3 Labour
Labour hours needed for January = 9,000 × 0.5 = 4,500
Labour hours available = 2,000 × 25/12 = 4,167
Labour cost = (4,167 × £9) + ((4,500 – 4,167) × £11) = £41,166

(c)

Operating budget	First draft	Alternative scenario	Working
Sales price £ per unit	6.00	6.54	6 × 1.09
Sales volume	90,000	81,900	90,000 × 0.91
	£	£	
Sales revenue	540,000	535,626	6.54 × 81,900
Costs:			
Materials	190,000	172,900	190,000 × 0.91
Labour	150,500	136,955	150,500 × 0.91
Water	16,666	16,826	16,666/1.04 × 1.05
Depreciation	7,000	6,500	W1
Total	364,166	333,181	
Gross profit	175,834	202,445	
Increase/(decrease) in gross profit		26,611	

Working

1 Depreciation is in steps of 6,500 by volume. Therefore the charge at volume of 90,000 puts this at the 14th step. Each step is therefore £7,000 ÷ 14 = £500.

A volume of 81,900 ÷ 6,500 = 12.6, ie the 13th step. £500 x 13 = £6,500.

Task 6

(a)

Description	Term
A financial measure of the difference between budget and actual performance	Variance

(b)

Direct labour costs		Favourable/ Adverse
Flexed budget (standard cost)	£72,000 W1	
Actual labour cost per hour (correct to £0.01)	£18.66 W2	
Actual labour hours per unit (correct to 2dp)	0.44 hrs W3	
Rate variance	£2,310 W4	Adverse
Efficiency variance	£9,000 W5	Favourable
Cost variance	£6,691 W6	Favourable
Cost variance % (correct to one decimal place)	9.3% W7	

Workings

1 = No of units produced × standard usage × standard price = 8,000 × 0.5 × 18 = £72,000

2 = Total labour cost / total labour used = 65,309/3,500 = £18.66

3 = Total labour used / no of units produced = 3,500/8,000 = 0.44 hrs

4 = (Standard rate – actual rate) × actual labour hours = (18.00 – 18.66) × 3,500 = 2,310

5 = (Standard hours – actual hours) × standard cost (4,000 – 3,500) × £18 = 9,000

6 = Flexed budget cost – actual cost = £72,000 – £65,309 = £6,691 (small rounding difference)

7 = Cost variance / flexed budget cost = 6,691 / 72,000 = 9.3%

(c)

Direct materials cost statement	£
Standard direct materials cost of production	1,064,800 *W1*
Materials price	91,960 *W2*
Materials usage	145,200 *W3*
Materials cost	237,160 *W4*

Workings

1. 880,000 ÷ 2,000 = £440
   £440 × 2,420 = £1,064,800

2. Standard price = 880,000 ÷ 44,000 = £20/kg
   Actual price = 827,640 ÷ 45,980 = £18/kg
   Materials price variance = (£20 – £18) × 45,980 = £91,960
   Variance is favourable – price is lower than budget.

3. Standard usage = 44,000 ÷ 2,000 = 22kg/unit
   Actual usage = 45,980 ÷ 2,420 = 19kg/unit
   Materials usage variance = (22 – 19) × £20/kg × 2,420 = £145,200
   Variance is favourable – usage is lower than budget (fewer kgs per unit).

4. Standard cost of 2,420 units = 2,420 × 22kg × £20 = £1,064,800
   Actual cost of 2,420 units = £827,640
   Variance = £1,064,800 – £827,640 = £237,160 (Favourable)

Task 7

Operating budget		Flexed budget	Actual	Variance Fav/(Adv)
120,000	Sales volume (units)	140,000	140,000	
£		£	£	£
6,000,000	Sales revenue (W1)	7,000,000	6,720,000	–280,000 A
	Costs			
1,080,000	Material (W2)	1,260,000	1,313,680	–53,680 A
660,000	Labour (W3)	770,000	782,310	–12,310 A
150,000	Production managers (W4)	200,000	192,000	8,000
24,000	Distribution (W5)	28,000	35,281	–7,281 A
250,000	Energy (W6)	280,000	296,530	–16,530 A
30,000	Equipment hire (W8)	30,000	30,000	0
414,000	Depreciation	414,000	412,000	2,000 F
332,000	Marketing and advertising	332,000	315,320	16,680 F
529,000	Administration	529,000	534,200	–5,200 A
202,000	Other production overheads (W7)	219,000	212,300	6,700 F
3,671,000	Total costs	4,062,000	4,123,621	–61,621 A
2,329,000	Operating profit	2,938,000	2,596,379	–341,621 A

Workings

1. Sales £6,000,000/120,000 = £50 per unit, so flexed budget is 140,000 × £50 = £7,000,000
2. Materials £1,080,000/120,000 = £9 per unit, so flexed budget is 140,000 × £9 = £1,260,000
3. Labour £660,000/120,000 = £5.50 per unit, so flexed budget is 140,000 × £5.50 = £770,000

4 Production managers: 120,000/45,000 = 2.67, so 3 production lines were budgeted to be in operation requiring 2 production managers each. This is six in total at £150,000/6 = £25,000 each. When production is 140,000 units, 140,000/45,000 = 3.11 ie 4 production lines in operation and 8 production managers are needed, at a cost of 8 × £25,000 = £200,000.

5 Distribution £24,000/120,000 = £0.20/unit. Flexed budget: 140,000 × £0.20 = £28,000

6 Energy variable element: 120,000 × £1.50 = £180,000, so fixed element is £250,000 – £180,000 = £70,000. Therefore flexed budget this year is (140,000 × £1.50) + £70,000 = £280,000

7 Production overheads: fixed element = £100,000 therefore variable element = (£202,000 – £100,000)/120,000 = £0.85. Therefore flexed budget this year is (140,000 × £0.85) + 100,000 = £219,000

8 Equipment hire is a stepped cost, but original and flexed budget are in the same range so flexed budged = £30,000.

Task 8

To:	Managing Director	**Date:**	(Today)
From:	Budget Accountant	**Subject:**	**Reasons for variances and actions**

Reasons for variances

Sales variance

As the budget has been flexed, prices were lower than expected per unit. This may have reflected discounting if the brand image had suffered due to quality issues.

Materials variance

There is an adverse materials variance due to the increase in prices by the key supplier. Our attempt to source cocoa from alternative suppliers led to quality problems and so we used more cocoa than expected (adverse usage variance in addition to adverse price variance).

Labour variance

This was partly due to the machine breakdown, when staff were unable to work, but also due to the staff unrest because of the stoppage of free chocolate to staff. Staff were therefore both paid for work when they were idle, and were less efficient because they were less motivated.

Fixed production overheads

The use of specialist engineers to fix the machinery will have contributed to the adverse fixed overheads variance.

Actions

If we cannot source a reliable, cheaper supplier of cocoa then the standard cost of material should be increased in the next budget, to reflect the prices charged by the key supplier.

No amendment should be made to the standards used in the budget in relation to labour, as both occurrences (staff go-slow and machine breakdown) are hopefully not to be repeated.

If not, for example if the breakdown is indicative of the machinery becoming less reliable, it may be necessary to budget for higher maintenance costs within fixed production overheads in future.

If we have had to reduce prices permanently because of image problems, we should amend the standard selling price in the next budget.

BPP PRACTICE ASSESSMENT 3 MANAGEMENT ACCOUNTING: BUDGETING

Time allowed: 2.5 hours

PRACTICE ASSESSMENT 3

Management Accounting: Budgeting BPP practice assessment 3

Task 1 (20 marks)

(a) Match the information with an appropriate source which will provide, or help you forecast, that information when constructing a budget. (6 marks)

(CBT instructions: Click on a box in the left column, then on one in the right column. To remove a line, click on it.)

Information required
Foreign exchange rates
National Insurance Contribution rates
Interest rates on factory mortgage
Sales demand of a new product
Irrecoverable debts
Directors' bonuses

Source
Market research consultant
HM Revenue & Customs website
Credit controller
Loan agreement
Articles of Association of Company
Board minutes
The Financial Times

(b) Who would you contact in each of the following situations?

(CBT instructions: Click on a box in the left column, then on one in the right column. To remove a line, click on it.) **(4 marks)**

Situation
You want to explain a materials usage variance
You want your budget to be authorised
You want to explain a materials purchases variance
You want to obtain details of promotional activity for a product

Pick from
Purchasing department
Managing director
Sales department
Production manager
Budget committee

(c) Select an appropriate accounting treatment for each of the following costs: **(7 marks)**

Expenditure	Accounting treatment
Material wastage	▼
Companies House penalty for late filing	▼
Food and drink at opening of new showroom	▼
Cost of purchasing manager	▼
Room hire for office staff training course	▼
Material storage costs	▼
Machinery maintenance costs	▼

Picklist:

Activity-based charge to production cost centres
Allocate to administrative overheads
Allocate to marketing overheads
Charge to production at a machine hour overhead rate
Direct cost

(d) Select the appropriate term to match the following description.
(1 mark)

Description	Term
An area of the business which incurs costs, but also generates income	▼

Picklist:

Absorption costing
Investment centre
Marginal costing
Profit centre

(e) Calculate a sales revenue forecast for year 5.

Do not show decimals. *Round to the nearest whole pound.*

Use the sales price index to calculate sales revenue for years 1 to 4 at year 1 prices.
(2 marks)

	Year 1 Actual	Year 2 Actual	Year 3 Actual	Year 4 Actual
Sales revenue (£)	12,200	12,747	13,527	14,091
Sales price index	110.0	114.0	120.0	124.0
Sales revenue at year 1 prices (£)				

Task 2 (20 marks)

Closing inventory is to be 20% of the next period's sales. Sales in period 4 will be 12,000 units.

(a) Complete the following production budget in units for the product. (11 marks)

	Period 1	Period 2	Period 3
Opening inventory	2,200		
Production			
Subtotal			
Sales	11,000	11,500	11,700
Closing inventory			

The next three months' production budget is shown below. Of the completed units, 2% fail a quality test and are scrapped.

(b) How many units must be manufactured to allow for the scrapped units? (3 marks)

	Month 1	Month 2	Month 3
Required units	18,000	20,000	15,000
Manufactured units			

A product uses a material P in its production. P costs £3 per litre. The materials purchasing budget for material P in the next quarter is being constructed. The budgeted production is 5,000 units in the next quarter.

Each unit of product uses 0.75 litres of P, but a further 0.05 litres is lost in wastage for every unit made. There will be inventory levels of 345 litres of P at the start of the quarter, but inventory of only 150 litres is required at the end of the quarter.

(c) What is the materials purchasing budget (in £) for the coming next quarter? (2 marks)

Select from:

	✓
£3,805	
£4,195	
£11,415	
£12,585	

A company makes two products, A and B, using the same grade of labour. The company pays 10 employees for a 35 hour week, regardless of whether all hours are worked, at a rate of £10 per hour. Overtime is paid at £12 per hour.

Product A requires 0.5 labour hours

Product B requires 2 labour hours

The budgeted production for the next four week period is

Product A 500 units

Product B 500 units

(d) What is the labour cost budget for the next four week period? **(2 marks)**

Select from:

	✓
£12,500	
£12,600	
£14,000	
£16,100	

(e)

Budgeted sales of Product P for the next quarter are 42,000 units.

Finished goods in inventory at the start of the quarter are 7,000 units and closing inventory will be 8,334.

The standard cost card indicates that each unit should take 3.5 labour hours. However, it is anticipated that, due to technical problems, during the quarter the workforce will only be working at 92% efficiency.

The production budget for the quarter is [ ] units. **(1 mark)**

The labour usage budget for the quarter is [ ] hours. **(1 mark)**

Task 3 (20 marks)

(a) You are required to complete the following working schedules and operating budget for production of 16,000 units.

(9 marks)

Working schedules

Materials

	Kg	£
Opening inventory	500	1,000
Purchases	2,400	6,000
Sub-total	2,900	7,000
Usage		
Closing inventory	450	

Closing inventory of raw material is to be valued at budgeted purchase price.

Labour

	Hours	£
Basic time @ £15 per hour		
Overtime		
Total		

Each unit takes six minutes. There are 1,400 basic labour hours available. Overtime is paid at time and a half.

Overhead

	Hours	£
Variable @ £0.80 per hour		
Fixed		4,000
Total		

Variable overhead recovered on total labour hours.

(b) Now complete the operating budget. **(6 marks)**

	Units	£
Sales @ £2.40 each	15,000	
Opening inventory	–	
Cost of production	16,000	
Materials		
Labour		
Production overhead		
Total production cost		
Closing inventory of finished goods	1,000	
Cost of goods sold		
Gross profit		

Closing inventory of finished goods is valued at budgeted production cost per unit.

(c) Complete the cash flow forecast using the budget data that you have calculated in parts (a) and (b) of this task and the additional information below. **(5 marks)**

Enter receipts and payments positive figures.

- Receivables will increase by £2,500.
- Materials payables will increase by £1,750.
- Labour costs are paid in the period in which they are incurred.
- Payables for production overheads will reduce by £1,400.
- A new machine was acquired at a cost of £25,000 in the month, which will be paid for a month in arrears.

Cash flow forecast	£	£
Opening balance/(overdraft)		5,334
Sales receipts		
Payments:		
Materials		
Labour		
Production overheads		
Capital expenditure		
Total payments		
Closing cash balance/(overdraft)		

Task 4 (20 marks)

You have been responsible for preparing a cash budget. An extract is given below showing cash inflows.

Cash budget

	This year's actual cash inflows £	Next year £
Cash inflows from sales	185,000	179,000
Proceeds from sale of car		14,000

You have constructed the budget with reference to this year's cash inflows and the following information.

Sales are expected to remain constant. Receivables at the end of this year are £30,000. Historically, year-end receivables are kept at this level but they are expected to increase by 20% by the end of next year.

The managing director's car is sold every two years at a loss of around £10,000, and replaced with a better model.

The managing director is concerned that sales appear to be decreasing in this cash budget, and asks for an explanation regarding the car sale.

Write an email to the Managing Director explaining the calculations and assumptions in your cash budget. Address his concern regarding sales and the car transaction. **(20 marks)**

To:	Managing Director	**Date:**	(Today)
From:	Budget Accountant	**Subject:**	**Cash Budget inflows**

Sales

Car

Task 5 (20 marks)

(a) Select the appropriate term to match the description.

(2 marks)

Description	Term
The difference between the actual amount spent on materials compared to the budgeted amount spent on materials	▼
A budget that is constantly updated to cover the next 12 month period	▼

Picklist:

Bottom up budgeting
Incremental budgeting
Material price variance
Material usage variance
Performance indicator
Performance review
Rolling Budget
Top down budgeting
Total material cost variance
Variance
Variance analysis
Zero based budgeting

The following budget has been constructed for a year.

	Budget for the year	Budget for month 1
Sales forecast (units)	200,000	16,000
Production budget (units)	180,000	14,000
	£	£
Sales	900,000	
Materials used	270,000	
Labour	36,000	
Variable production overhead	180,000	
Variable selling overhead	100,000	
Fixed overheads	58,000	

Material, labour and variable production overheads are variable with the number of units produced.

Variable selling overheads vary with units sold.

Fixed overheads are incurred evenly throughout the year.

(b) Complete the budget for month 1. **(6 marks)**

You have submitted a draft operating budget to the budget committee. The committee has asked you to budget for an alternative scenario and calculate the increase or decrease in expected profit.

(c) Complete the alternative scenario column in the operating budget table and calculate the increase or decrease in profit. **(12 marks)**

Assumptions in the first scenario

Material and labour costs are variable.

Depreciation is a stepped cost, increasing at every 7,000 units.

There is an allowance for an energy price rise of 5%.

Alternative scenario

Increase the selling price by 4%.

Reduce the sales volume by 12%.

Revise the energy price rise to 3%.

Apart from sales price per unit, do not enter decimals.

***Round to the nearest whole number*, if necessary.**

Operating budget	First draft	Alternative scenario
Sales price £ per unit	12.00	
Sales volume	50,000	
	£	£
Sales revenue	600,000	
Costs:		
Materials	212,500	
Labour	202,250	
Energy	16,275	
Depreciation	9,600	
Total	440,625	
Gross profit	159,375	
Increase/(decrease) in gross profit		

Task 6 (20 marks)

(a) Select the appropriate term to match the description.

(2 marks)

Description	Term
A method of budgeting that takes last year's budgeted figure and adjusts for any change in activity level; and inflation	▼

Picklist:

Bottom up budgeting
Incremental budgeting
Rolling Budgets
Top down budgeting
Zero based budgeting

(b) Complete both the tables to show the variances of actual performance against budget, and then actual performance against flexed budget. **(10 marks)**

The materials and labour costs are variable costs, the production overhead is a fixed cost and the general expenses are a semi-variable cost with a fixed element of £13,600.

	Budget 28,000 units £	Actual 31,500 units £	Variances Fav/(Adv) £
Sales	406,000	441,000	
Materials	165,200	180,400	
Labour	100,800	115,600	
Production overhead	37,500	39,000	
Gross profit	102,500	106,000	
General expenses	55,600	68,900	
Operating profit	46,900	37,100	

	Flexed budget 31,500 units £	Actual 31,500 units £	Variances Fav/(Adv) £
Sales		441,000	
Materials		180,400	
Labour		115,600	
Production overhead		39,000	
Gross profit		106,000	
General expenses		68,900	
Operating profit		37,100	

(c) Prepare the direct labour cost statement from the activity data provided. **(8 marks)**

Enter favourable variances as positive figures – for example 500.

Enter adverse variances as negative figures – for example –500.

Activity data	Items produced	Labour hours	Cost (£)
Budget	48,000	372,000	2,604,000
Actual results	50,000	385,000	2,810,500

Direct labour cost statement	£
Standard direct labour cost of production	
Variances (adverse shown as negative)	
Labour rate	
Labour efficiency	
Labour cost	

Task 7 (20 marks)

The budgeted and actual performance for a month is given below.

Flex the budget to the actual activity level, given the information below about costs, and show whether each variance is favourable or adverse. (20 marks)

Enter favourable variances as positive figures – for example 500.

Enter adverse variances as negative figures – for example –500.

	Budget	Flexed budget	Actual	Variance Fav/(Adv)
	100,000	120,000	120,000	
	£	£	£	£
Sales revenue	4,500,000		4,865,000	
Material	2,200,000		2,437,500	
Labour	500,000		518,000	
Equipment hire	12,000		25,000	
Distribution	33,000		35,600	
Light, heat, power	72,000		90,000	
Depreciation	100,000		90,000	
Administration	220,000		230,000	
Marketing	180,000		190,000	
Profit	1,183,000		1,248,900	

- Material and labour costs are variable.
- The cost for light, heat and power is semi-variable. The budgeted fixed element is £22,000.
- The budget for marketing costs is stepped, increasing every 80,000 units.
- Depreciation and administration costs are fixed.
- Distribution costs are semi-variable. The budgeted variable elements are £0.30 per unit.
- The budget for equipment hire costs is stepped, increasing every 20,000 units.

Task 8 (20 marks)

Operational review

Review the operating statement shown and the additional information below, and prepare a report by email.

Additional information

At the end of the previous year a new warehouse had been purchased which has meant a saving in warehouse rental.

Six new machines were installed at the start of the year which are more power-efficient than the old machines, but also more expensive, causing a larger depreciation charge.

There was an unexpected increase in the materials price during the year and when other suppliers were contacted it was found that they were all charging approximately the same higher price for the materials.

A higher than normal skilled grade of labour was used during the year due to staff shortages. The production process is a skilled process and the benefit has been that these employees, although more expensive, have produced the goods faster and with less wastage. This particular group of employees is also keen to work overtime and, as the business wishes to build up inventory levels, advantage of this has been taken.

The original budget was prepared by a management committee and approved by the Chief Executive. She is pleased that profit is higher than originally budgeted, but asks you how she can encourage the management team to perform even better in the future.

Operating statement	Flexed budget	Actual	Variance Fav(Adv)
Sales volume		21,300 units	
	£000	£000	£000
Sales revenue	**670**	**680**	**10**
Variable costs			
Material	185	205	(20)
Labour	92	94	(2)
Distribution	30	30	–
Power	15	15	–
Equipment hire	78	79	(1)
Total	400	423	(23)
Contribution	**270**	**257**	**(13)**

Operating statement	Flexed budget	Actual	Variance Fav(Adv)
Fixed costs			
Power	70	40	30
Depreciation	15	35	(20)
Rent	70	48	22
Marketing	25	25	–
Administration	20	20	–
Total	200	168	30
Operating profit	**70**	**89**	**19**

Write an email to the chief executive, in three parts, in which you explain:

(a) (i) What effect the combination of the factors given above might have had on the fixed costs, materials and labour variances from the flexed budget.

(ii) Any action that should be taken in light of these factors.
(10 marks)

(b) The steps that should be taken when setting budgets, if they are to be successful in motivating staff. **(5 marks)**

(c) Why managers should be held responsible for controllable costs only. **(5 marks)**

To:	The Chief Executive	**From:**	Budget Accountant
Subject:	**Review of Operating Statement**	**Date:**	xx.xx.xx

(a) Effect of factors on variances

(b) Steps if budgets are to motivate

(c) Controllable costs

BPP PRACTICE ASSESSMENT 3 MANAGEMENT ACCOUNTING: BUDGETING

ANSWERS

Management Accounting: Budgeting BPP practice assessment 3

Task 1

(a)

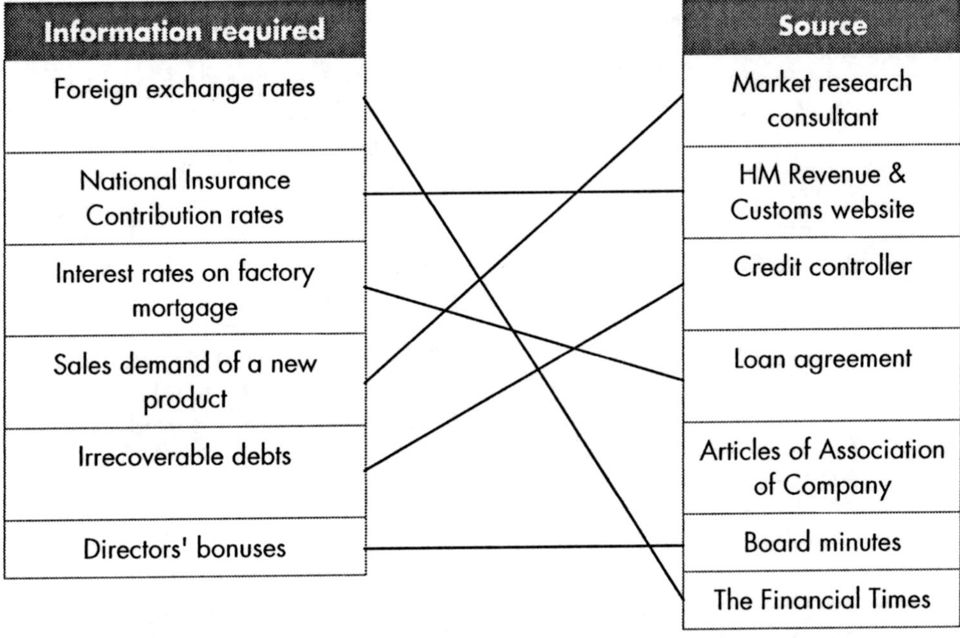

(b)

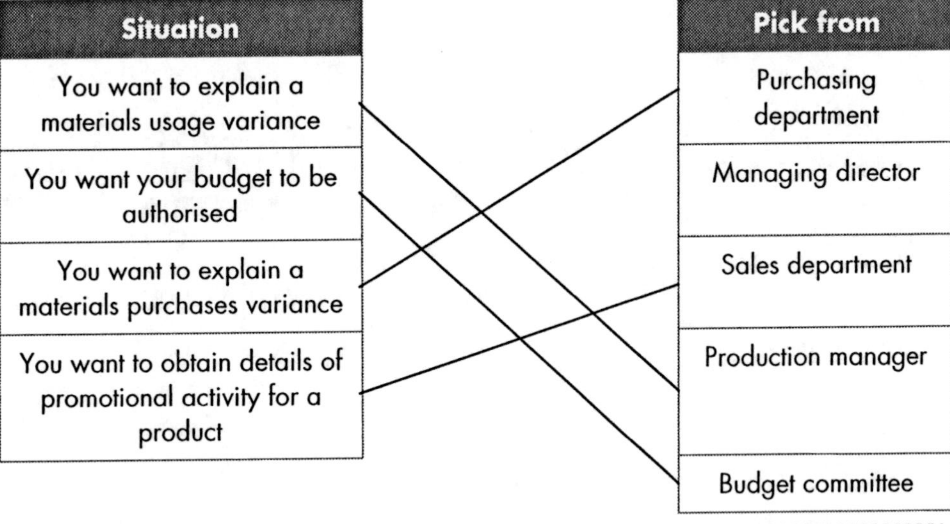

(c)

Expenditure	Accounting treatment
Material wastage	Direct cost
Companies House penalty for late filing	Allocate to administrative overheads
Food and drink at opening of new showroom	Allocate to marketing overheads
Cost of purchasing manager	Activity-based charge to production cost centres
Room hire for office staff training course	Allocate to administrative overheads
Material storage costs	Activity-based charge to production cost centres
Machinery maintenance costs	Charge to production at a machine hour overhead rate. (Or – activity-based charge to production cost centres)

(d)

Description	Term
An area of the business which incurs costs, but also generates income	Profit centre

(e)

	Year 1 Actual	Year 2 Actual	Year 3 Actual	Year 4 Actual
Sales revenue (£)	12,200	12,747	13,527	14,091
Sales price index	110.0	114.0	120.0	124.0
Sales revenue at year 1 prices (£)	12,200	12,300	12,400	12,500

Workings

Year 2: $£12,747 \times \frac{110}{114} = £12,300$

Year 3: $£13,527 \times \frac{110}{120} = £12,400$

Year 4: $£14,091 \times \frac{110}{124} = £12,500$

Task 2

(a)

	Period 1	Period 2	Period 3
Opening inventory	2,200	2,300	2,340
Production	11,100	11,540	11,760
Subtotal	13,300	13,840	14,100
Sales	11,000	11,500	11,700
Closing inventory	2,300	2,340	2,400

Workings

Closing inventory:

20% × 11,500 = 2,300

20% × 11,700 = 2,340

20% × 12,000 = 2,400

Production = sales + closing inventory – opening inventory

Period 1 production = 11,000 + 2,300 – 2,200 = 11,100

Period 2 production = 11,500 + 2,340 – 2,300 = 11,540

Period 3 production = 11,700 + 2,400 – 2,340 = 11,760

(b)

	Month 1	Month 2	Month 3
Required units	18,000	20,000	15,000
Manufactured units	18,368	20,409	15,307

Workings

18,000 × 100/98 = 18,368 etc – must be rounded up to ensure sufficient units are made after 2% are scrapped

(c)

	✓
£3,805	
£4,195	
£11,415	✓
£12,585	

Workings

Material usage = budgeted production × budgeted usage per unit (including wastage)

= 5,000 × (0.75 + 0.05)

= 4,000 litres

Materials purchases (litres) = closing inventory + usage – opening inventory

= 150 + 4,000 – 345

= 3,805 litres

Materials purchase (in £) = £3 × 3,805 = £11,415

(d)

	✓
£12,500	
£12,600	
£14,000	✓
£16,100	

Workings

Labour hours required for budgeted production:

Product A 500 × 0.5 = 250 hours

Product B 500 × 2 = 1,000 hours

Total hours required = 250 + 1,000 = 1,250 hours

Hours available without overtime = 10 × 35 × 4 weeks = 1,400 hours

Therefore no overtime is required, but the company must pay for 1,400 hours at £10 per hour = £14,000

(e)

The production budget for the quarter is [43,334] units.

The labour usage budget for the quarter is [164,858] hours.

Workings

Production budget – units

Sales quantity	42,000
Less opening inventory	(7,000)
Add closing inventory	8,334
Production quantity	43,334

Labour usage budget – hours

Hours required	
43,334 × 3.5 × 100/92	164,858 hours

Task 3

(a)

Working schedules

Materials

	Kg	£
Opening inventory	500	1,000
Purchases	2,400	6,000
Sub-total	2,900	7,000
Usage	2,450	5,875
Closing inventory (450 × £6,000/2,400)	450	1,125

Labour

	Hours	£
Basic time @ £15 per hour	1,400	21,000
Overtime	200	4,500
Total	1,600	25,500

Overhead

	Hours	£
Variable @ £0.80 per hour	1,600	1,280
Fixed		4,000
Total		5,280

(b)

Operating budget

	Units	£
Sales @ £2.40 each	15,000	36,000
Opening inventory	0	0
Cost of production	16,000	
Materials		5,875
Labour		25,500
Production overhead		5,280
Total production cost		36,655
Closing inventory of finished goods	1,000	2,291
Cost of goods sold		34,364
Gross profit		1,636

Workings

Materials

Usage = opening inventory + purchases – closing inventory = 2,450 kg

Cost of closing inventory = £6,000/2,400 × 450 = £1,125

Usage price is the balance of £7,000 – £1,125 = £5,875

Labour

Time for production = 16,000 × 6/60 = 1,600 hours, therefore 200 overtime hours are required.

1,400 @ £15 per hour = £21,000

200 @ £15 × 1.5 = £4,500

Overheads = £0.80 × 1,600 = £1,280

Closing inventory = total production cost/16,000 × 1,000 = £2,291

Deduct from total production cost to give cost of sales £36,655 – £2,291 = £34,364

(c)

Cash flow forecast	£	£
Opening balance/(overdraft)		5,334
Sales receipts		33,500
Payments:		
Materials	4,250	
Labour	25,500	
Production overheads	6,680	
Capital expenditure	0	
Total payments		36,430
Closing cash balance/(overdraft)		2,404

Workings

1 Sales receipts = Revenue – change in receivables = 36,000 – (2,500) = £33,500

2 Materials payments = Material cost – change in payables = 6,000 – 1,750 = £4,250

3 Production overheads = Cost – change in payables = £5,280 – (–1,400) = £6,680

4 Capital expenditure = £Nil, as paid in the next month

Task 4

To:	Managing Director	**Date:**	(Today)
From:	Budget Accountant	**Subject:**	**Cash Budget inflows**

Sales

I have prepared the cash budget by considering the change in receivable balances at the start and end of next year. Receivables are expected to increase by 20%, ie (£30,000 × 1.2) to £36,000. Sales are not decreasing but are expected to be the same as last year. However, as receivables will increase by £6,000 we will collect £6,000 less cash than the sales we actually make.

Last year, there was no change in the receivables balance at the start and end of the year, so the cash collected from sales was therefore equal to those sales (£185,000).

Assuming the same level of sales, and the £6,000 increase in receivables, means we will collect £185,000 – £6,000 = £179,000.

Car

We buy and sell a car for you every two years. The current carrying amount (net book value) of the car in the accounts is £24,000, but it is assumed that we will sell this for a £10,000 loss as in previous years, so the actual proceeds received will be £14,000 as shown in the cash budget.

The extract you have is of the cash inflows only. You need to look at the full cash budget which will show the outflow of cash for the new car being purchased.

Task 5

(a)

Description	Term
The difference between the actual amount spent on materials compared to the budgeted amount spent on materials	Total material cost variance
A budget that is constantly updated to cover the next 12 month period	Rolling budget

(b)

	Budget for the year	Budget for month 1
Sales forecast (units)	200,000	16,000
Production budget (units)	180,000	14,000
	£	£
Sales	900,000	72,000
Materials used	270,000	21,000
Labour	36,000	2,800
Variable production overhead	180,000	14,000
Variable selling overhead	100,000	8,000
Fixed overheads	58,000	4,833

Workings

1 Sales

Sales price per unit = £900,000/200,000 = £4.50 per unit

Therefore, sales of 16,000 units = £4.50 × 16,000 = £72,000

2 Materials

Materials cost per unit produced (using annual budget) = £270,000/180,000 = £1.50 per unit

Material cost of 14,000 units in month 1 = 14,000 × £1.50 = £21,000

3 Labour

Labour cost per unit produced (from annual budget) = £36,000/180,000 = £0.20

Labour cost of 14,000 units in month 1 = 14,000 × £0.20 = £2,800

4 Variable production overhead

Variable production overhead per unit (from annual budget) = £180,000/180,000 = £1.00 per unit

Variable production overhead costs for month 1 = 14,000 × £1.00 = £14,000

5 Variable selling overheads

Variable selling overheads per unit (from annual budget) = £100,000/200,000 = £0.50 per unit

Variable selling overheads for month 1 = 16,000 × £0.50 = £8,000

6 Fixed overheads

For month 1, fixed overhead = 58,000/12 = £4,833

(c)

Operating budget	First draft	Alternative scenario	Working
Sales price £ per unit	12.00	12.48	12 × 1.04
Sales volume	50,000	44,000	50,000 × 0.88
	£	£	
Sales revenue	600,000	549,120	12.48 × 44,000
Costs:			
Materials	212,500	187,000	212,500 × 0.88
Labour	202,250	177,980	202,250 × 0.88
Energy	16,275	15,965	16,275/1.05 × 1.03
Depreciation	9,600	8,400	W1
Total	440,625	389,345	
Gross profit	159,375	159,775	
Increase/(decrease) in gross profit		400	

Working

1 Depreciation is in steps of 7,000 by volume. Therefore the charge at volume of 50,000 puts this at the 8th step. Each step is therefore £9,600 ÷ 8 = £1,200.

A volume of 44,000 ÷ 7,000 = 6.29, ie the 7th step. £1,200 × 7 = £8,400.

Task 6

(a)

Description	Term
A method of budgeting that takes last year's budgeted figure and adjusts for any change in activity level; and inflation	Incremental budgeting

(b)

	Budget 28,000 units £	Actual 31,500 units £	Variances £
Sales	406,000	441,000	35,000 (F)
Materials	165,200	180,400	15,200 (A)
Labour	100,800	115,600	14,800 (A)
Production overhead	37,500	39,000	1,500 (A)
Gross profit	102,500	106,000	3,500 (F)
General expenses	55,600	68,900	13,300 (A)
Operating profit	46,900	37,100	9,800 (A)

	Flexed budget 31,500 units £	Actual 31,500 units £	Variances £
Sales	456,750	441,000	15,750 (A)
Materials	185,850	180,400	5,450 (F)
Labour	113,400	115,600	2,200 (A)
Production overhead	37,500	39,000	1,500 (A)
Gross profit	120,000	106,000	14,000 (A)
General expenses (W)	60,850	68,900	8,050 (A)
Operating profit	59,150	37,100	22,050 (A)

Working

General expenses:

At 28,000 units – Variable element = £55,600 – 13,600/28,000
= £1.50 per unit

At 31,500 units:	£
Variable element 31,500 × £1.50	47,250
Fixed element	13,600
Total cost	60,850

(c)

Direct labour cost statement	£
Standard direct labour cost of production	2,712,500 W1
Variances (adverse shown as negative)	
Labour rate	–115,500 W2
Labour efficiency	17,500 W3
Labour cost	–98,000 W4

Workings

1 2,604,000/ 48,000 = £54.25

£54.25 × 50,000 = £2,712,500

2 Standard rate = 2,604,000/ 372,000 = £7.00/hr

Actual rate = 2,810,500/385,000 = £7.30/hr

Labour rate variance = (£7 – £7.30) × 385,000 = –£115,500

Variance is adverse – rate is higher than budget

3 Standard efficiency = 372,000 ÷ 48,000 = 7.75hrs/unit

Actual efficiency = 385,000 ÷ 50,000 = 7.70hrs/unit

Labour efficiency variance = (7.75 – 7.70) × £7/hr × 50,000 = £17,500

Variance is favourable – efficiency is better than budget (fewer hours per unit)

4 Standard cost for 50,000 units = 50,000 × 7.75hrs × £7.00 = £2,712,500

Actual cost for 50,000 units = £2,810,500

Variance = £2,712,500 = £2,810,500 = £98,000 (Adverse)

Task 7

	Budget	Flexed budget	Actual	Variance Fav/(Adv)
	100,000	120,000	120,000	
	£	£	£	£
Sales revenue (W1)	4,500,000	5,400,000	4,865,000	(535,000) A
Material (W2)	2,200,000	2,640,000	2,437,500	202,500 F
Labour (W3)	500,000	600,000	518,000	82,000 F
Equipment hire (W6)	12,000	14,400	25,000	(10,600) A
Distribution (W7)	33,000	39,000	35,600	3,400 F
Light, heat, power (W4)	72,000	82,000	90,000	(8,000) A
Depreciation	100,000	100,000	90,000	10,000 F
Administration	220,000	220,000	230,000	(10,000) A
Marketing (W5)	180,000	180,000	190,000	(10,000) A
Profit	1,183,000	1,524,600	1,248,900	275,700 F

Workings

1 Budgeted selling price per unit

Revenue/sales volume
£4,500,000/100,000 = £45
Flexed budget: 120,000 × £45 = £5,400,000

2 Budgeted material cost

£2,200,000/100,000 = £22
Flexed budget: 120,000 × £22 = £2,640,000

3 Budgeted labour cost

£500,000/100,000 = £5
Flexed budget: 120,000 × £5 = £600,000

4 Budgeted light, heat, power cost

Fixed element = £22,000
Original budget, variable element = £72,000 – £22,000 = £50,000
Variable element per unit = £50,000/100,000 = £0.5 per unit
Flexed budget variable element 120,000 × £0.5 = £60,000
Total flexed cost = £22,000 + £60,000 = £82,000

5 Budgeted marketing cost is stepped, but original and flexed budget in the same range so flexed budget = £180,000.

6 Budgeted equipment hire is a stepped cost, increasing every 20,000 units.

100,000/20,000 = 5 steps

£12,000/5 steps = £2,400 per step. So 120,000 requires 6 steps, ie £2,400 × 6 = £14,400

7 Distribution variable element: 100,000 × £0.30 = £30,000, so fixed element is £33,000 – £30,000 = £3,000. Therefore flexed budget this year is (120,000 × £0.30) + £3,000 = £39,000

Task 8

To:	The Chief Executive	**From:**	Budget Accountant
Subject:	**Review of Operating Statement**	**Date:**	xx.xx.xx

(a) Effect of factors on variances

I have reviewed the results for the period. There was an operating profit of £89,000, compared with a flexed budget profit of £70,000. This represents a favourable variance of £19,000.

New warehouse – this will have the effect of reducing the rent expense but increasing the depreciation expense. The favourable rent expense variance of £22,000 appears to be a result of this.

New machines – the new machines use less power than the old ones, and therefore reduce the power expense. This appears to have resulted in a favourable power variance of £30,000. There will, however, be an increase in the depreciation charge as a result of the new machines.

Taken together, both the new warehouse and the new machines have contributed to the adverse depreciation variance of £20,000. Each of these changes has individually resulted in favourable variances (£22,000 and £30,000) that are greater than the combined adverse depreciation variance, so the changes both appear to have been beneficial.

Once the reduction in rent and power costs and the increase in depreciation charge are known, then the standard fixed overhead should be adjusted.

Price increase – the price increase will be a cause of the adverse materials variance. The price increase appears to be a permanent one as all suppliers have increased their prices so the standard materials cost should be altered.

Skilled labour – the use of the higher skilled labour would be expected to have a favourable effect on the labour efficiency variance. The additional expense of the skilled labour and the overtime that has been worked will have had an adverse effect on the labour rate variance, which has cancelled out the effect of the increased labour efficiency to leave a small adverse labour variance. Unless the use of this grade of labour is likely to be a permanent policy then there should be no change to the standard labour rate or hours.

The use of the higher skilled labour would also have a favourable effect on the materials variance due to decreased wastage. However, the adverse effect of the increased price much exceeds this positive effect on materials, leading to the £20,000 adverse variance.

(b) Steps if budgets are to motivate

Managers should participate in setting the budgets.

The budgets should be agreed with all parties.

Targets should be challenging but attainable.

All known external (non-controllable) factors should be included in the forecasts.

Managers should be appraised only on costs within their budget which they can control.

Budgets should be reviewed during the period to which they relate, and revised for factors beyond the control of managers.

(c) Controllable costs

Operations managers can only be held responsible in the short term for variances arising from their own decisions, rather than from factors outside their control such as inaccuracies in overall planning.

If costs, revenues and variances are reported as part of the responsibility of a manager but in fact he or she has no control, then this can have a de-motivational effect.

Looking at the operating statement, for example, if an operations manager were to be assessed on the basis of the adverse materials variance, then this would likely be de-motivational as the cause of that adverse variance lay outside of that manager's control.